# REGION
# LOCKED

Special thanks to

**Patron**
Sam Street

# REGION LOCKED

## DID YOU KNOW GAMING?

unbound

First published in 2021
Unbound
Level 1, Devonshire House, One Mayfair Place, London, United Kingdom, W1J 8AJ
www.unbound.com

Text Design by PDQ Digital Media Solutions Ltd
A CIP record for this book is available from the British Library
ISBN 978-1-78352-926-1 (trade hbk)
ISBN 978-1-78352-927-8 (ebook)
Printed in Slovenia by DZS Grafik

1 3 5 7 9 8 6 4 2

# Contents

With thanks to

**Superfriends**
Selwyn Alcantara
Ahmed Alrashed
Stuart Ashen
Jared Burns
Sophie Chapman-Smith
Callum Clarke
Caleb Kopp
Samuel 'Captain Anchorbeard' Langley
Peter Lawrence
Jonathan Lindblom Vestin
James Mahy
Bryan 'Malkavio' Mason-McCaw
Brandon Oakes
Linh Pham
Yishay Shapira
Vitas Varnas
Frank Wilson

# INTRODUCTION

Hello, and welcome to *Region Locked*... the book!

We three boys from Norfolk are huge fans of the wide array of video games published across the globe, but being from a rural part of the UK, we were subject to the restrictions that came with video game publication back in the day. Since our youth, things have certainly made a change — the expansion of the Internet and global trade has meant that our ability to experience games that were previously out of our grasp has become less of a mission.

Through the collaboration of many translators and hackers online, some games are now even more accessible than ever — having translations into multiple languages they otherwise would have never received, enabling players to not only understand a game's dialogue, but also appreciate themes that would have otherwise been missed, such as historical and cultural references. While this book will concentrate on a more English-centric audience, translation communities online have been doing this for multiple languages found all over the world, increasing the accessibility to players around the globe.

Throughout this book, we'll talk about games that had releases without any English, some that have since been translated by fans online, or unusually, some that actually did find their way into English translation, though were not published within the United States — an anomaly in standard release practices, as the United States has the biggest English-speaking audience in the world.

The name of this book, and the series on YouTube it is based upon, *Region Locked*, comes from a practice in game publication that has died out in more recent years. Traditionally, many consoles had variations created for different regions around the world — often being programmed to only boot games published within the same region the system was sold in, or simply having a different form of physical cartridge that would not fit into a console sold in another country. When a game from one country is released which won't boot within a console made for another, it is considered a 'Region Locked' game.

We hope that this book will give you a greater look into the history of games, but remember to not treat it as some sort of 'recommended playing list' — simply because a game is in these pages and we've looked into it, does not mean that it was some lost masterpiece. Attempting to play every game we list would be time-consuming, disheartening, expensive, and above all, it would put us out of a job.

Dazz, Greg and Matt

# THE ADVENTURE OF LITTLE RALPH

CONSOLE:      SONY PLAYSTATION
YEAR:         1999
DEVELOPER:    NEW CORPORATION
PUBLISHER:    ERTAIN CORPORATION, NEW
              CORPORATION
REGION:       JAPAN

Japan has a large quantity of platformers that never left the region, but typically these games were made during the 8-bit and 16-bit eras. 2D platformers became less common after the PlayStation's release, as games tried making use of the console's 3D capabilities. One 2D platformer America never received was *Chippoke Ralph no Daibouken*, otherwise known as *The Adventure of Little Ralph*. *The Adventure of Little Ralph* was released for the PlayStation in 1999, and was developed by New Corporation, a team with few projects to its name. The title's gameplay and style are reminiscent of the arcade era of platformers, and people often think the game is an arcade port. However, *Little Ralph* was created exclusively for the PlayStation.

The game follows Ralph, an eighteen-year-old orphan. When his village is attacked by a demon army known as the Lost Clan, Ralph tries to defend it. However, he comes up against the leader of the clan, the powerful Valgo, a demon obsessed with his own muscles. Valgo casts a spell that strips Ralph of his gear and turns him into a child, but before Valgo manages to throw the finishing blow, Ralph's childhood friend Luticia shows up to protect him. Unleashing a powerful magic ability she'd kept hidden all those years, Luticia saves Ralph — but is instead kidnapped by Valgo. Naked and helpless, Ralph finds a magical holy sword on the battlefield that guides him to save his friend and defeat the Lost Clan.

The game works like a typical action

Greg:
*The Adventure of Little Ralph* is not only a great game to peel your eyes at — it's also a great game to play. The platforming and swordplay are challenging but not frustrating, interchanging with the one-on-one versus battles that will give a warm wave of *Street Fighter* nostalgia. That said, the end boss, Valgo, is borderline total BS and will make you want to tear your arm off and throw it at the television.

platformer, with Ralph being able to run, jump and swing his sword. Ralph can pick up a shield that grants him one additional hit before he dies, and also find power-ups for his sword, which widen his range, or cause fireballs to shoot from his sword when it swings. Along the way, Ralph can find a small animal friend, Feirio, that helps him by throwing explosives.

The game uses a score system, and points are gained by collecting fruit or killing enemies. Points can also be multiplied by charging Ralph's sword attack. Ralph will then use it like a bat, knocking enemies in a straight line into one another and multiplying the points earned.

Initially, the game's boss battles must be undertaken as young Ralph. About halfway through the game, however, Ralph gains the power to temporarily turn back into an adult during boss battles. When he does this, the game switches genres and the boss battles become similar to a fighting game. Specifically, the gameplay is close to a classic *Street Fighter* title, with less concentration on combos and more on performing special attacks. It isn't particularly complex compared to most standalone fighting games, but it offers an interesting twist as the game progresses.

After completing the game, a new versus mode is unlocked, which allows you to play as Ralph or the bosses against a friend. Other elements expand the replay-ability too. For example, the player can't get the full ending on easy difficulty, which features only five levels compared to the normal mode's eight. We'll refrain from talking about the true ending for those who wish to play the game themselves.

*The Adventure of Little Ralph* received a widely positive response, with reviewers finding the 2D graphics and flow admirable for the time of release. Many also felt it was

fairly hard, even on the easiest setting. game's seamless transitions between lev were highly praised; it cleverly hid loadin screens by showing an animation of Ral entering the next stage.

*The Adventure of Little Ralph* began l as a Sharp X68000 home computer title The game only moved to the PlayStatio after the X68000 became redundant, an this is likely why the game has a very re feel. In 1999, video games were moving away from simplistic 2D platformers, ins opting for flashy 3D graphics and new s of gameplay. In contrast, Ralph's origins apparent with its points and lives system Games released in the late nineties norr forgo a score system entirely and use a system instead of lives and continues. C interesting feature is found in the option menu, where the game's sound mode ca be set to PSG, reminiscent of older audio chips instead of the higher quality audio found in PlayStation games.

ST5-1 3:36 ♥×4 ×4/6 376700

ST5-2 4:38 ♥×4 ×4/6 428300

## Localisation

There are a few reasons why *Little Ralph* never came to the West when it was first published. That being said, there's no official response for which reason is most accurate. As explained before, this game wasn't intended to push the PlayStation's hardware, and was instead a throwback to the days of platform gaming. When Sony was designing the original PlayStation, they were convinced 3D was the future after seeing SEGA's *Virtua Fighter* in action. This belief shaped not only the PlayStation's hardware, but which games appeared on the platform.

In the West, many people wanted to see the latest and greatest in gaming technology, which usually meant the most cutting-edge 3D graphics. Sony shared this mentality, at least in the West, and limited the amount of 2D games that appeared on its platforms. This made it difficult for developers who wanted to localise their 2D games for the Western market. One of these developers is SNK's Yoshihito Koyama, who was the director of Japan/US relations on many 2D SNK titles. In 2004, Koyama told SPOnG.com, 'Sony just isn't interested in 2D games anymore — whatever it might be. [...] And yet many games, as long as they are in

3D, trickle through all the time. It's a crazy situation and we don't believe it reflects the needs of game consumers.'

*Little Ralph* was released in 1999, not too long before Koyama made this statement. It wouldn't be hard to imagine how this mentality would stop a 2D PlayStation game coming to Western shores at the turn of the millennium. To add fuel to the fire, the companies involved in developing and publishing *Little Ralph* were both very small, and to this date have never had an international release. They would have lacked the power and experience necessary to deal with Sony's stance on 2D.

Another reason for the game's lack of localisation could be that in 1999, we were eagerly awaiting Sony's next big console, the PlayStation 2. They might have thought bringing a game from an unknown brand to a dying platform wasn't worth the risk.

Curiously, while researching *Little Ralph*, we discovered its official website is not only presented in Japanese, but also English. This could suggest the game was intended at one point to be brought to the West, perhaps at the same time as it was distributed online in Japan as a digital download for the Japanese PlayStation store in 2007.

# ALTERED BEAST

| | |
|---|---|
| CONSOLE: | SONY PLAYSTATION 2 |
| YEAR: | 2005 |
| DEVELOPER: | SEGA |
| PUBLISHER: | SEGA |
| REGION: | JAPAN, EUROPE |

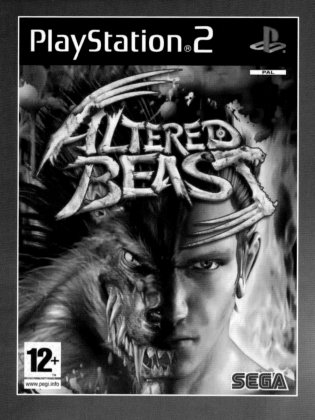

SEGA's history is full of games that are considered arcade classics, and some of these were made even more popular by their home console ports. 1988's *Altered Beast* is seen by many as one of SEGA's standout titles. It follows the story of a centurion resurrected by Zeus, who is instructed to go forth and rescue Zeus's daughter, Athena, from the demon lord Neff. To do this, the centurion can transform into a number of creatures, like a werewolf, by collecting power-ups.

The game's original arcade ending reveals that the characters in the game are actually actors fulfilling the roles for a film production.

For America, the arcade game — and its ports — would be the only *Altered Beast* titles released. For Europe and Japan, on the other hand, there was an *Altered Beast* game released on the PlayStation 2.

The game follows Luke Custer, a man who is a 'Genome Cyborg'. His DNA has been artificially modified so that he can make use of microchips containing the genes of different beasts, allowing him to transform into various anthropomorphic creatures. At the start of the game, Luke crash lands on an island after the helicopter transporting him is attacked. He loses his memory and must learn the truth about himself and the experiment that was carried out on him.

**Greg:**
Don't be fooled by this game. Yes, the transformation sequences are spectacularly violent and inventive, but the game is about two bin bags from a full-on garbage fire. The combos are clunky, the movement is stiff, the camera is unreliable and the environments are painfully boring, not to mention that the story is a huge wet turd. We note that the game has very little in common with the original and it couldn't be more true. What's the word for the opposite of an absolute classic?

Over time we learn that Luke is a special military operative, sent to investigate a genetic outbreak in a small coastal town.

Set across an open and explorable island divided into smaller locations, the player must make their way through each area while defeating enemies and obtaining additional DNA samples. Combat is primarily focused on combos and transformations, with Luke being able to switch between each transformation at any time through the use of the circle button. This allows him to become a variety of different creatures, with the werewolf being the primary focus of the game.

The player has two different energy bars: one for their health, and one which determines the amount of time they can remain in their transformed state. After this second energy bar is depleted, the player's health will begin to rapidly decline in its place.

To top the bar up, the player must defeat monsters and collect green or red energy that spawns on their corpses. Green is for more monster energy, and red for more health. This encourages the player to kill many enemies in quick succession so that they can stay transformed for longer periods of time. By killing enemies, it's possible to increase the volume of combos that can be performed for each transformation. Additional skills can also be learned at certain points, like improving the jump height of the werewolf, which helps the player navigate the map and gain entrance to previously inaccessible locations.

Upon completion, additional forms can be used in New Game+, giving the player

a total of nine different beasts to transform into. These are:

**The Werewolf:** Used for fast combos and as a general all-round fighter.

**The Merman:** Can navigate deep water. His only attack is a homing torpedo.

**The Wendigo:** Delivers strong, slow punches and can lift heavy objects. With slow movement, his abilities are better utilised against larger creatures.

**The Garuda:** Provides the ability to move around the map with its flying capability. This form is also able to attack from a distance.

**The Minotaur:** Takes the appearances of a flaming bull. Able to burn enemies with both fists and horns.

**The Dragon:** Considered to be the ultimate genome transformation in the game's plot.

Able to use lightning-based attacks to defeat enemies, with devastating effect.

The additional forms that can be unlocked after completing the game are:

**The White Weretiger:** Plays like a slightly stronger version of the werewolf.

**The Grizzly Bear:** Uses various earth attacks to deliver massive damage.

**The Unidentified Weightless Human (UWH):** Capable of controlling gravity and time. Able to kill enemies instantly and deliver massive damage to bosses.

The game's plot and character have very little in common with SEGA's original release. The two games only share the similar theme of a character transforming into a variety of beasts. Gameplay, plot, characters and environment have all been changed, looking to create a more modern setting from that of Ancient Greece.

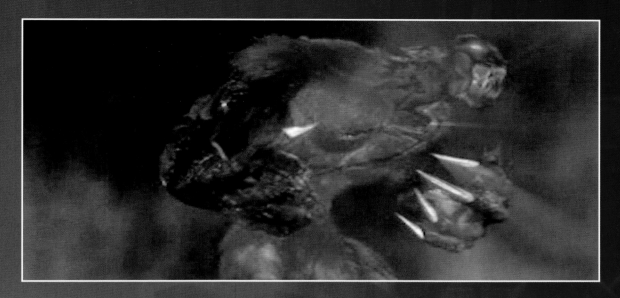

## Localisation

The game received mostly negative reviews on release, with many claiming the title holds little value for those who weren't already fans of the original game. Poor controls and a lack of cohesive plot led to this negative reception, and ultimately damaged the game further when it came to localisation.

In a 2004 article, it was revealed that SEGA had cancelled efforts to bring the title to the US market. The lack of positive response to the game likely caused SEGA to cut their losses. While this isn't confirmed, we also believe that the violent imagery of the transformations that play every time the player turns into a different beast form may have concerned the American marketers. However, with that said, the European release surprisingly received an age rating of only 12.

# BAHAMUT LAGOON

**CONSOLE:** NINTENDO SUPER FAMICOM,
NINTENDO WII, NINTENDO WII U
**YEAR:** 1996, 2009 (WII), 2014 (WII U)
**DEVELOPER:** SQUARE
**PUBLISHER:** SQUARE
**REGION:** JAPAN

Developed by Square in 1996, rereleased on the Wii in 2009, and rereleased once more on Wii U in 2014, *Bahamut Lagoon* puts the player in the role of Byuu. In the sky world of Orelus, Byuu is the former captain of the renowned Kahna Dragon Squad and now the leader of a rebel group called the Resistance. The story begins with Byuu failing to protect his childhood friend, Princess Yoyo. When she's kidnapped by the Granbelos Empire, led by Emperor Sauzer, it means more than just losing a princess — it means world domination.

You see, Princess Yoyo is capable of awakening ancient dragons, a power the enemy is making use of. It's Byuu's job to uncover the legends of the holy dragons, bring peace back to the world by awakening their awesome power, and take down the tyrannous Sauzer.

King Kahna: Daughter...
Can you sense Bahamut?

The game broke many role-playing game (RPG) storytelling conventions at the time, providing insight into the villains and their relationships with one another. Non-playing characters (NPCs) throughout the game look upon your liberative actions as having negative impacts. Many people live under Sauzer's rule happily, feeling the world has been united under him and peace achieved.

The gameplay is like most strategy RPGs of its time. The player moves units on a grid-based map into locations where they can perform attacks and skills on their opponents. The player raises dragons for use in battles, and so must choose how to raise them to better perform in fights. If the player is unable to beat their enemy in a fight, they can save their experience from the battle and try again, allowing them to get stronger with each defeat. Units are made up of a selection of dragons and their dragon-handlers, providing bonuses with like-for-like skills and stat attributes.

Making use of a map's terrain is pivotal to success in battles. Map features can be used to the player's advantage and disadvantage. For example, bridges can be destroyed

while units are on them, causing the units to drown. To combat this, the player can cast ice on water to form a solid platform for the units to stand on.

Upon entering battle with an enemy, the gameplay switches to the turn-based battle system Square and *Final Fantasy* are known for. One interesting element of *Bahamut Lagoon*'s battle system is how dragons change the way these battles play out. The dragons have their own minds and will randomly attack the enemy to provide support when they see fit. When an enemy is killed by a magical attack of a certain element, it increases the chances of item

drops related to the element used. These drops can be used to further advance the stats and skills of the player's arsenal of dragons.

The game was widely praised for its developed characters, who had their own personalities and plot lines. Its unique spin on combat was also well received, with its mix of tactical planning and standard Japanese role-playing game (JRPG) gameplay.

Members of the *Final Fantasy* staff worked on the game, including supervision by *Final Fantasy* creator Hironobu Sakaguchi and story planning from Motomu Toriyama. The game was directed by Kazushige Nojima, writer of future titles *Final Fantasy 7* and its spinoffs, *Final Fantasy 8*, and the *Kingdom Hearts* series. *Bahamut Lagoon* to this date is one of Nojima's only credits as director.

These connections to *Final Fantasy* provide interesting insight into *Bahamut Lagoon*'s development. Evidence shows the incorporation of many elements from *Final Fantasy* into *Bahamut Lagoon* were likely made because *Bahamut Lagoon* was intended to be part of the *Final Fantasy* series. While we're unable to verify this, it's often said during development the game went under the working title of *Final Fantasy Tactics*. It was a year after the release of *Bahamut Lagoon* before the name *Final Fantasy Tactics* was used for a title officially released on the original PlayStation.

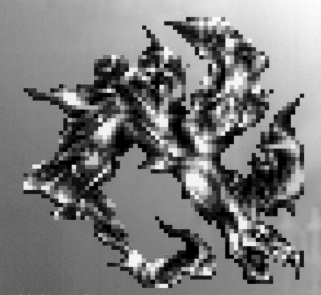

## Localisation

*Bahamut Lagoon* remains exclusive to Japan, having been released in the region three times. With no official translation available, the only way of playing the game in English is with the unofficial translation patch provided by DeJap Translations in a joint effort between translators Neill Corlett and Tomato. Many believe Square's reluctance to release the title outside Japan was due to their belief there was a lack of interest in RPGs in the Western market, with the exception of the *Final Fantasy* series.

This lines up with several other actions by the company around this time, such as publishing other games which saw no localisation, changing the name of games when taken to the West to incorporate the *Final Fantasy* name, and creating an RPG specialised for the Western market. *Final Fantasy Mystic Quest* was that game, an extremely watered-down RPG that resulted from Square's belief that RPG mechanics were too complex for Western audiences at the time.

As *Bahamut Lagoon* was a new intellectual property (IP), Square may have considered an English translation a fruitless venture. This mentality likely changed as the gaming market grew and Square saw huge success with other titles in the Western market. Sadly, this change occurred too late for much of the company's already published library, and thus those games remain region locked.

# BATTLE GOLFER YUI

**CONSOLE:** SEGA MEGA DRIVE
**YEAR:** 1991
**DEVELOPER:** SANTOS
**PUBLISHER:** SEGA
**REGION:** JAPAN

*Battle Golfer Yui* was developed by Santos, an obscure company with very few major releases under their belt prior to their merger with SEGA's internal research and development team.

The game follows the story of Yui Mizuhara, a high school student and golfer. Yui and her best friend Ran Ryuzaki are kidnapped by Professor G, the leader of Dark Hazard. This is because they are the ideal candidates for cybernetic enhancements that will transform them into battle-ready powerhouses known as battle golfers, which Professor G plans to use in order to (somehow) take over the world. Before his plans can play out and Yui is brainwashed, she is rescued by a mysterious man in a lab coat and set free.

Seeking to learn more about what has happened, after hearing nothing for several days, she learns of a golf tournament sponsored by the Hazard Foundation. She voluntarily enters herself into the contest to find the truth, her friend Ran, and the man who rescued her. On her journey, Yui will encounter many combatants, all of which refer to her as 'Black Fire'; like her, they are battle golfers. The player must defeat each opponent in a best of three; however, a draw is also counted as a loss. Defeating each battle golfer will grant the player new skills and experience points as well as uncovering more information and progressing the story. A defeat is an instant game over.

The player is able to speak with characters before and after each

**Greg:**
*Battle Golfer Yui* has aged surprisingly well. When playing I found that the charming and bizarre humour, as well as fun twist on the standard golf game, made it almost impossible to stop. Beware though, the CPU players can be incredibly unforgiving, so expect a struggle. However, there's nothing quite as satisfying as fire-blasting a ball to send it spinning and weaving to an outrageous hole-in-one.

"Can you walk?
The exit is over there! Hurry, go!"

match as well as think, observe and sometimes collect or use items, in a similar fashion to graphic adventure games.

Many players have pointed out that each battle golfer appears to be a parody of a character from popular Japanese media. Hagata is a reference to Hanagata from the popular baseball manga *Kyojin no Hoshi* — he even refers to Yui as 'Hoshi'. Kitako appears to be a female version of Kitarō from the popular manga *GeGeGe no Kitarō*. In the manga, Kitarō has one eye covered with his hair — this is because not only is his eyeball missing but it's actually inhabited by the ghost of his father and lives on his head. Similarly, Kitako has one eye covered, except the missing eyeball is her mother. And finally, Dibot is a parody of the title character of the 1977 Japanese superhero series *Kaiketsu Zubat*.

The golf gameplay plays like many standard golf titles of the time. The player can select a club, where they will hit the ball and in which direction, and a sliding power gauge determines the driving force. There is also wind that impacts the drives with varying direction and force. The player can also check

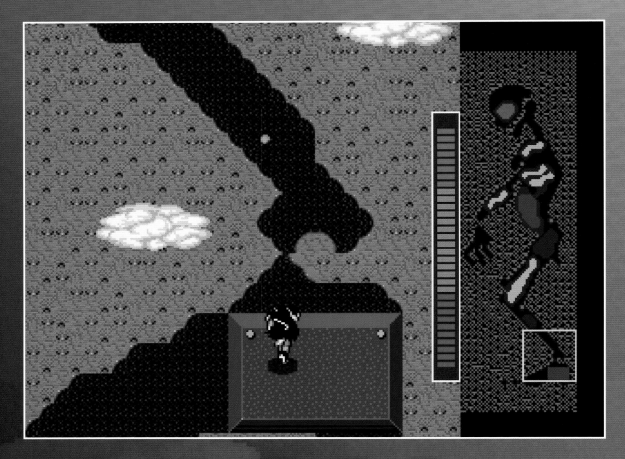

with their caddie to find out the distance to the pin and the condition of the terrain.

As previously mentioned, unlike most golf games, skills can be unlocked and used to cause different effects to the player's shot; for instance, making the ball stop dead when landing, allowing the ball to skim on the surface of water and even a power that lets the player control the direction of the ball in mid-air. Each of these skills costs SP (skill points), with the player's maximum SP being increased by earning experience and levelling up.

Unlike standard golf, many of the game's courses are fantastical — such as a baseball pitch or a graveyard — and therefore feature a variety of shapes and hazards. The game makes use of passwords, allowing for a number of cheats. According to the game's fan translator, Filler, these were originally

haikus, including two popular Japanese haikus by one of the most famous poets of the Edo period, Matsuo Bashō:

Title: 古池や蛙飛びこむ水の音

Translation: 'The Old Pond'

'Ah! The ancient pond,
as a frog takes the plunge,
    sound of the water'

Title: 夏草や兵どもが夢の跡

Translation: 'Summer Grass'

'Mounds of summer grass
the place where
noble soldiers one time dreamed a dream'

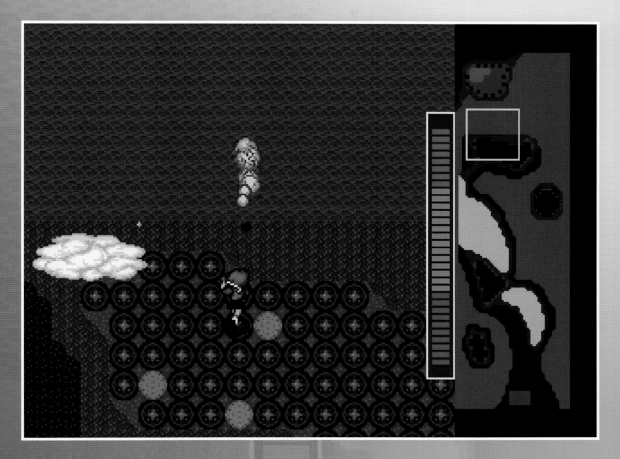

And lastly, the original developers included their own haiku:

'Stroke
Since there are skills. It is easy'

There is also a two-player mode in which players can compete across the game's courses, utilising the entire arsenal of skills acquired throughout the adventure.

**SPOILER ALERT!** During Yui's investigation, she enters a hidden lab and encounters Doctor T, the man who rescued her during the game's introduction. He reveals that he is the brother of Professor G, and though he attempted to thwart his brother's efforts at world domination, it was too late. He then puts it upon Yui to defeat Professor G and utters a cryptic message — 'When flame and Thunderbolt Unite...' — before he is killed with a golf ball.

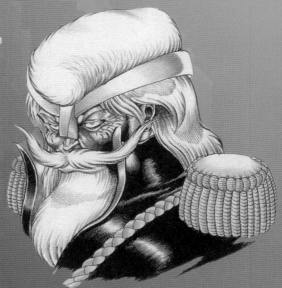

Yui must then face off against Professor G. He explains that he created the tournament to train Yui to become the ultimate battle golfer. Once defeated he goes on to clarify that this is because he wanted somebody to replace him as the head of Dark Hazard due to his impending death, after his cybernetic enhancements shortened his lifespan. His plan was to have Yui and Ran face off to decide his successor. Before leaving, the player searches G's body and finds a mysterious flute.

In an unsurprising twist, seeing as Dibot just outright tells the player of the fact earlier in the game, it is revealed that Ran — now known as 'Shadow Thunder' — has been acting as Yui's golf caddie for the entire game.

Yui must then defeat Ran in a golfing match. These battles feature the starting course of each of the other opponents the player defeated, alternating with a set of new courses for the final showdown.

After winning the showdown, Yui tries desperately to remind Ran of who she once was; however, it seems as though she is not easily turned. Yui then remembers the flute she acquired from Professor G.

Here the player is faced with two options: blow the flute or destroy it. Each decision leads to a different ending. If the player decides to blow the flute, the voice of Professor G echoes through Yui's mind and she becomes Dark Fire, taking up the mantle of leader for Dark Hazard. The player then receives a game over. On the other hand, if the player decides to destroy the flute, the mental conditioning on Ran is broken and she is returned to her former self. Unfortunately, as Yui offers her hand to help Ran up from the ground, Flame finally meets Thunderbolt and a huge explosion is triggered, killing 20,000 people and injuring many more. The player then sees Yui and Ran travelling up a tall lift overlooking the city. THE END.

## Localisation

A large number of reasons behind the game's lack of localisation can be determined. *Battle Golfer Yui* combined two genres which weren't popular with publishers of Mega Drive games in the West: golf and RPGs. The game received generally poor reception amongst Japanese reviewers, giving SEGA a good indication that the title would fare badly with an overseas audience.

However, in 2007, ROMhacking.net user 'Guest' posted initial groundwork on tools to translate the title. Building upon this effort, users Supper and Filler got to work on finishing a patch to not just translate the game into English, but also fix a number of bugs present in the original. Rather than attempt to localise the game for familiarity's sake with Westerners, much of the game's references remain as they were in order to preserve the game's original script.

Speak            Anger

Ask                              STATUS

▶ Check                          LV            3

Think                            SP           15

                                 EXP          20

| GUEST: | 'GURU LARRY' BUNDY JR. |
|---|---|
| CONSOLE: | COMMODORE 64 |
| YEAR: | 1984 |
| DEVELOPER: | MASTERTRONIC |
| PUBLISHER: | MASTERTRONIC |
| REGION: | EUROPE |

You can tell this is a British video game a mile off because of the UK's bizarre obsession with heroic octogenarians, with other titles such as *Super Gran* and *Ninja Grannies*. But Mastertronic's 1984 budget title, *Bionic Granny*, is quite possibly gaming's cardinal coffin-dodging protagonist (though 'antagonist' is probably the optimum word here). She also has the dubious accolade of being the first female protagonist in a British-developed video game!

Now, if the concept of playing as an old age pensioner doesn't sound ludicrous enough, the entire premise of *Bionic Granny* is that you linger outside primary schools at home time waiting for the kids to come out, where you then assault as many children as possible with your 'laser-powered brolly' as they desperately try to escape your wrath down back alleys. Your only true enemy in the game is a lollipop lady who is trying to shoo you off with her stick. However, brutalise enough younglings, and you move on to the next comprehensive.

Even more bizarrely, when you die in the game, you fall on the floor and the enormous head of Spider-Man explodes out of your chest. Seriously! Also, I've no bloomin' clue what the relevance of her being a cyborg actually is to the game, but then again, we've seen how stupid the *Terminator* franchise has become nowadays; it wouldn't surprise me if *Bionic Granny* is regarded as an official spin-off!

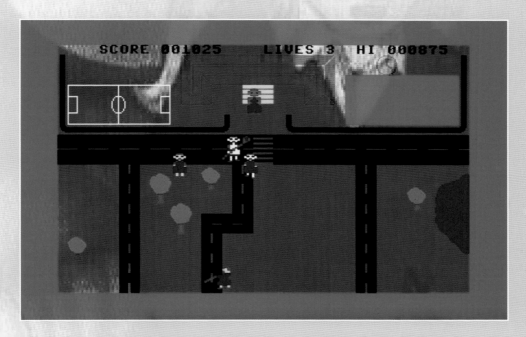

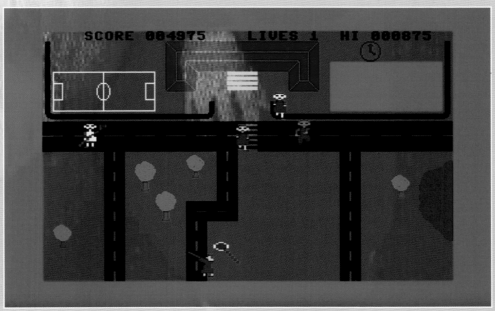

# BOMBERMAN HARDBALL

**CONSOLE:** SONY PLAYSTATION 2
**YEAR:** 2004
**DEVELOPER:** HUDSON SOFT
**PUBLISHER:** UBISOFT
**REGION:** JAPAN, EUROPE

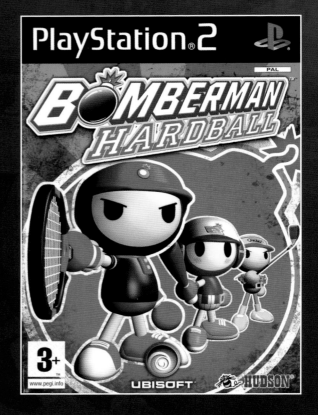

*Bomberman*: a series that has been around from the early days of gaming. Its history spans a large catalogue of games, ranging from the expected to the unexpected; from internationally recognised classics to region-locked obscurities. As with most recognised characters in the gaming world, it should come as absolutely no surprise to see Bomberman pull out the sweat bands and take on a sports genre in *Bomberman Hardball*.

*Bomberman Hardball* was first released in Japan as *Bomberman Battles* in 2004, before a PAL version was released a year later. While most *Bomberman* games take the form of a competitive top-down action game, Hudson decided to take the series into a different form of competition.

Split up in four games, the title includes three different sports as well as the traditional Battle Mode as seen in standard *Bomberman* games. Another mode is also present which provides the most interesting element to the game, called Living Mode.

Living Mode shows the white bomber in his house. The house contains a small variety of things to explore. Through the use of a remote, the player can watch demos of the different game modes, played by only the game's CPU players. It's also possible to select an option to customise the player's character, name them and purchase new outfits from a gumball machine with coins earned through the

The game's modes are pretty much what you would expect.

Baseball has two modes: a single match, or a pennant race with the player entering a league match against five CPU players over the course of thirty games. With the bulk of the game being controlled automatically — it's even possible to set the fielding to automatic — the game is mainly built around correctly timed button presses.

Golf can be played in both exhibition and tournament modes with eighteen different holes. Even if you've never played a golf game before, the game's mechanics are obvious. A power bar determines a shot's strength, and then stopping the bar at its stationary marker determines accuracy. It's

The Tennis Mode allows for exhibition matches and tournaments across both doubles and singles on grass, hard and clay courts. Again, this is merely a generic tennis game.

The game's main attraction is in its Battle Mode, the main gameplay of most other *Bomberman* releases. It follows the typical *Bomberman* formula of grid-based competitive action matches in which players attempt to blow each other up with bombs. The modes included are the classic deathmatch battles; star battles in which the player must collect the most stars; crown battles, where players hunt down a crown on the stage to win; and point battles, in which the player respawns upon death and points are awarded for each frag.

*Bomberman Hardball* was released with an English translation in PAL territories prior to the release of the *Bomberman Land* titles. As a result, several character names differ from other games within the series. Cheerful White is referred to as Ivory Bomber, Cool Black is named Star Bomber, Bookworm Green is called Jade Bomber and Kid Blue is Blue Bomber.

## Localisation
Ubisoft, *Bomberman Hardball*'s publisher, made a press release to announce the game's launch alongside *Bomberman* DS. The statement, from January of 2005, announces the company's intentions to 'publish and distribute *Bomberman* DS for the Nintendo DS in Europe and North America and *Bomberman Hardball* for Sony's PlayStation 2 throughout Europe'.

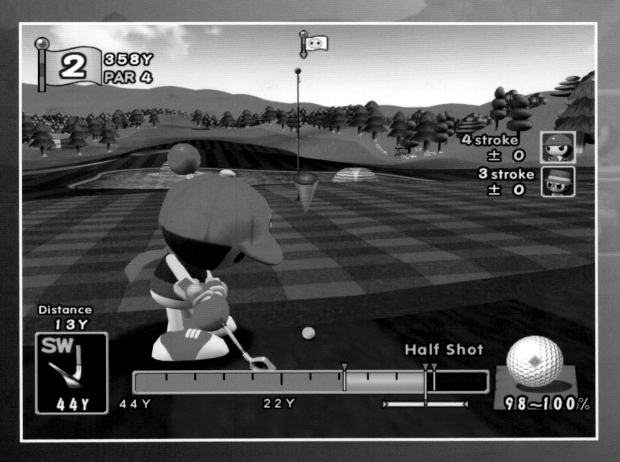

This reveals that, at the time of the game's announcement for international release, there were no intentions of the game being taken to the United States.

An anomaly with this *Bomberman* release is with the lack of Konami distribution. Ubisoft had likely signed an agreement with Hudson to publish the titles only a short period before Konami's acquisition of Hudson in April of 2005, three months before *Hardball*'s release.

The choice to release *Bomberman Hardball* outside of Japan but only in Europe is an oddity, with much of the game's materials and marketing focusing on the baseball element of the title, a sport which while not so popular in Europe, is particularly popular not only in Japan but in the US.

# BUSHI SEIRYŪDEN: FUTARI NO YŪSHA

**CONSOLE:** NINTENDO SUPER FAMICOM
**YEAR:** 1997
**DEVELOPER:** GAME FREAK
**PUBLISHER:** T&E SOFT
**REGION:** JAPAN

This Japanese gem comes from a company best known as the creators of *Pokémon* — Game Freak. The company also created another Japanese exclusive game featured in this book, *Mario & Wario*. But they had another game for the Super Nintendo that was never published in America: *Bushi Seiryūden: Futari no Yūsha*, which roughly translates as 'Warriors of the Blue Dragon Legend: The Two Heroes'.

Published in 1997 by T&E Soft, Game's Freak's *Bushi Seiryūden* is a unique blend of RPG genres. The player takes control of the game's protagonist in a fantasy-themed version of feudal Japan. While out adventuring, the hero encounters a small pink flying monster, Wokuu. Wokuu was once a girl, but has been transformed. It's her goal to find a way of reversing this transformation and becoming her true self once again. When the young swordsman's house is destroyed and his sister, Nami, is kidnapped by monsters, he seeks to rescue her.

The game's draw is in its unique gameplay. The player controls the hero

through several different perspectives. These include an overhead-style RPG like that of *The Legend of Zelda*. From

**Dazz:**
This game is beautiful; Game Freak's old-school style is clear.
The gameplay is also really solid. I personally believe that with
a bigger marketing push and international release, *Bushi Seiryūden*
would have had the potential for massive success. Possibly one of
my favourite games featured in this book.

this perspective you are able to navigate the world, visit towns, cut down grass, discover treasures and find dungeons. Talking to residents will initiate a first-person perspective, allowing you to look around the environment that surrounds the person you wish to speak with. And finally, entering a battle or dungeon will start a side-scrolling battle phase.

While the game appears to be an action game at first glance, this isn't actually the case. Battles are turn based and will only continue if the player moves or attacks. But rather than using a typical menu to work through these screens, the hero is directly controlled, as in a typical action game. Battles begin by either attacking an enemy on the overhead perspective, giving the player an advantage over them, or by being ambushed by the enemy, granting them an initial first strike. After a certain period of time, once the player is strong enough, weaker enemies can be wiped out directly from the overhead map. During battles, the player takes control

of not only the hero but also Wokuu. The hero is able to attack using a variety of sword techniques, or he can use a magical shield to defend himself. The shield is also capable of firing a bullet by using some of the player's kokoro meter, AKA spirit meter, but it will only deal half of the player's standard damage. Wokuu is able to assist the player by lifting him into the air for a short distance, allowing him to attack enemies that are out of reach. Wokuu can also distract some enemies and prevent them from hitting the protagonist. If knocked out, Wokuu can be revived after a number of turns or at the end of each fight.

The hero also has an ability known as the Heart Eye, allowing the player to learn more about the strengths of enemies as well as being able to find hidden paths. As the game progresses, other skills are

earned that help attack larger quantities of enemies or deal greater damage.

The main goal of the game is to destroy the tower of the Ocean God. The Ocean God was a god that turned evil, building a tower which connected heaven and earth. This created a path between the world of gods and the world of men, allowing for demons to invade. To destroy the tower, the player must obtain Magatama: small curved beads which were created as ceremonial and religious symbolic objects in the Kofun period of Japan. Visually, they appear to look similar to one half of the yin-yang symbol.

Each battle has a turn limit, indicated at the start of each fight. Winning the battle within the allotted number of turns provides the player with Magatama; the quicker the fight ends, the more Magatama obtained.

The most striking part of the game is its art, which is reminiscent of the Pokémon series. This is likely because *Bushi Seiryūden* was released just after the original Pokémon games, and had Pokémon artists Ken Sugimori and Motofumi Fujiwara work on the title, as well as Pokémon composer Junichi Masuda, who worked on the game's soundtrack. Also, and most notably, the game was designed and conceptualised by Pokémon creator Satoshi Tajiri.

## Localisation

*Bushi Seiryūden* was published near the end of the Super Nintendo's relevancy outside of Japan, with the Nintendo 64 having been released around the same time. The game's lack of localisation is probably linked to this late publishing date, as support of the Super Nintendo had begun to fizzle out by this point. Being an RPG, the game is also dialogue heavy. This would have increased the cost of translating the game and made the possibility of localisation even more remote. It's also worth noting that *Pokémon* still hadn't reached the West by this point, and Game

Freak weren't the internationally recognised developers they are today. Surprisingly, there is also no fan translation available online at the time of writing this.

The game was originally announced under the name *Magatama Densetsu*, translated as 'Magatama Legend', and several magazines claimed that the game was to be published by Enix. It appears that at some point in development, Enix dropped out of the contract due to concerns with the title's direction, and a deal was made with T&E Soft instead.

# CAPTAIN RAINBOW

**CONSOLE:** NINTENDO WII
**YEAR:** 2008
**DEVELOPER:** SKIP LTD.
**PUBLISHER:** NINTENDO
**REGION:** JAPAN

Skip Ltd. is a company best known for its work on the *Chibi-Robo!* series, which spans numerous Nintendo consoles. They're also known for their Art Style games for DSiWare and WiiWare. While the majority of these games were released internationally, skip developed a game that never quite made it to the West and has since become infamous online. *Captain Rainbow* was released in 2008 for the Nintendo Wii. The game's story follows Nick, a TV star in his homeland of Mameruca. Nick is famous for his alter-ego Captain Rainbow, a superhero whose weapon of choice is a magical yo-yo. However, new and different superheroes become the latest trend, and Nick's ratings start to plummet. In an attempt to regain his popularity, he travels to Mimin Island. Rafting across the ocean, Nick comes across a small animal struggling in the middle of the ocean. Heroically, he transforms into Captain Rainbow and dives in to save it. Unfortunately, however, water is Captain Rainbow's weakness, mostly because he can't swim, and Nick is separated from his rainbow belt, the source of his power.

Nick awakens on the shores of Mimin Island with the animal he tried to save alongside him. The mysterious creature then conjures a magical bangle around Nick's wrist. After seeing other creatures pick up his belt from the beach and make off with it, Nick follows them and discovers a small

**Matt Barnes:**
The way Nintendo managed to blend their classic bubbly style with adult jokes is incredibly impressive as it weirdly works. I played this for research and footage and had such a great time that I was pretty tempted to complete it. I would highly recommend finding a way to play it. Without any spoilers, after you grant the wishes, there is another section to the game that's worth playing, which we didn't talk about. Though it makes total sense why this wasn't released in the West, I do think we missed out on this oddball of a game. But maybe its charm comes from the fact we never got it...

village. There he meets Hikari, a girl who cares for the shrine on the island. She also has the ability to see into the future through visions. She tells him that visitors travel to the island to have their dreams come true; however, it has never actually happened. She goes on to explain that the person wearing the bangle is chosen by the stars, and only they can open the mysterious ancient stone door in the shrine and change the fate of the islanders.

Transform!    CAPTAIN☆RAINBOW

The player takes control of Nick as he attempts to befriend the people of Mimin Island by fulfilling tasks to help them achieve their dreams. He is awarded stars or 'sparklies' by completing a variety of tasks and minigames set out by the inhabitants, or through exploration of the island. In order to fulfil a wish, the player must first collect twenty sparklies. This process must be repeated for each character. All of the residents of Mimin Island are early Nintendo

characters who, for the most part, were relatively obscure at the time or lesser used within Nintendo's releases. Character locations and events change through a day/night cycle, requiring the player to be in specific locations at certain times. They include:

Hikari, who helps Nick when he first arrives on the island, is one of the protagonists of the Japanese exclusive Famicom Disk System title *Shin Onigashima*.

Takamaru, the protagonist from *The Mysterious Murasame Castle*, who wishes to be able to keep his composure around women.

Birdo, one of the few characters who reached a certain level of popularity within Nintendo releases, has come to the island to become attractive and popular with men.

The soldiers from the Japanese-exclusive game *Famicom Wars*, who seem to have given up their war-driven lives and instead express a wish to become professional volleyball players.

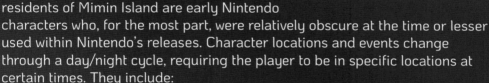

Little Mac, the protagonist of *Punch-Out!!*, who has let himself go physically. His desire is to train and become a world champion boxer once again.

Ossan, the playable character featured in the NES title *Golf*, often mistaken for Mario. He wishes to become a legendary golfer.

A number of references are spread throughout the game, including the use of warp pipes à la *Mario Bros.*, as well as portraits of both Mario and Link from *The Legend of Zelda* hanging over Tracy's throne.

Mappo and Tao, originating from the Japanese exclusive GameCube title *GiFTPiA*, but best-known for his main role in *Chibi Robo!* Mappo wishes to become a detective, and Tao wants nothing more than to eat as many bones as he can before he dies.

Lip, one of the playable characters from *Panel de Pon*, released as *Tetris Attack* internationally. Her desire is to become a great magician.

Tracy, who sells Link medicine in *The Legend of Zelda: Link's Awakening*. Bearing little resemblance to her earlier appearance in *Zelda*, her wish is to enslave all men in the world.

The Devil from *Devil World*, also a Japan and Europe exclusive title. His wish is to be the best villain in all of the underworld.

And lastly, Gitchoman from the *Chibi Robo!* series, who wishes to understand the difference between right and wrong.

To assist with his journey, Nick is able to transform into Captain Rainbow after recovering the rainbow belt, which will allow him to break rocks to clear paths as well as navigate the island faster with increased movement speed. While in his Captain Rainbow state, a power bar is displayed which will deplete over time. To keep the bar charged, the player must find food to consume; failing to do so will result in a game over.

Captain Rainbow's skills can be upgraded throughout the game by way of belt modifications.

The history of the island can be revealed by discovering rocks around the island, known as 'schists'. These provide more story and history surrounding the mysterious location. A number of collectables are also scattered around, such as animals which Nick is able to log in an animal encyclopaedia.

By granting the wishes of three people, the player is rewarded with access to their own portable caravan which can be moved by Captain Rainbow. In the caravan it's possible to save as well as to sleep to progress time, as opposed to having to go to Hikari's house to do so.

While *Captain Rainbow* received a lot of attention online, very little action was taken to bring the game across the pond for an international audience. Sales of the game were low, with only 6,361 copies being sold in the first week of release, though reviews seemed mostly positive, with Famitsu scoring the game thirty-one out of forty, praising the gameplay, pacing and musical score, though being put off by the often vulgar humour.

Many of the themes presented in *Captain Rainbow* can be considered lewd, such is the case with Birdo's story.

Birdo has been imprisoned in a cage by Mappo, after he found her in the women's bathroom, mistaking her for a man. This is a reference to Birdo's historically ambiguous gender. Birdo asks Nick to prove her innocence, leading him to search for an

> He won't listen to me, even
> if I kneel down.
> But I'll make him listen!

item that he can show to Mappo as proof.
This leads Nick to find an item which is only
shown as a question mark, found vigorously
vibrating underneath Birdo's pillow,
suggesting that the item is in fact a female
sex toy.

## Localisation

Low sales, controversial themes, and
region-exclusive obscure characters likely
gave Nintendo the impression that the title
wouldn't be a strong contender overseas
or could land them in hot water with
consumers.

    Despite this, a huge effort was taken by
the translation group Kirameki, with the
assistance of several other independent
translators. Kirameki first began showing
work on their translation in 2012, but after
years of work, no patch had been released.
While an almost fully translated script
had been created, the team were unable
to insert their translation into the game.
It wasn't until 2016 when ROMhacking.
net user MarkAss reinvigorated interest

in the project, ultimately
releasing an incomplete
patch in late 2017
using the original
script posted
by Kirameki.
This patch is
theoretically 95%
complete and makes
the game playable in
English.

# CHEESY

**GUEST:** CADDICARUS
**CONSOLE:** SONY PLAYSTATION
**YEAR:** 1996
**DEVELOPER:** CTA DEVELOPMENTS
**PUBLISHER:** OCEAN SOFTWARE, JALECO
**REGION:** EUROPE, JAPAN

See this game? Fuck it. Fuck Cheesy in his stupid Yellow-Bastard-Imitation face. If you don't live in Europe (or Japan), consider yourself lucky you never played this. Now, you may be wondering why on earth I harbour such negativity towards a seemingly innocent game about a yellow mouse, but one look at the cover followed by five minutes of playtime will make you understand why that is.

Published by Ocean Software and developed by CTA Developments for the PlayStation (the same masterminds behind *The Blues Brothers* and *Eek! the Cat* on Super Nintendo — I honestly wish I was making that up), the game began life as a project for the Atari Jaguar, moving to the PlayStation after the Jaguar became a commercial failure. Cheesy gives you an epic tale about a mouse kidnapped for genetic experiments — who then escapes from the lab after an alien attack. The game doesn't tell you this or explain it in the cutscenes, but that's as far as I can be arsed to analyse it.

As far as the game itself goes, it's a side-scroller with 3D models and the

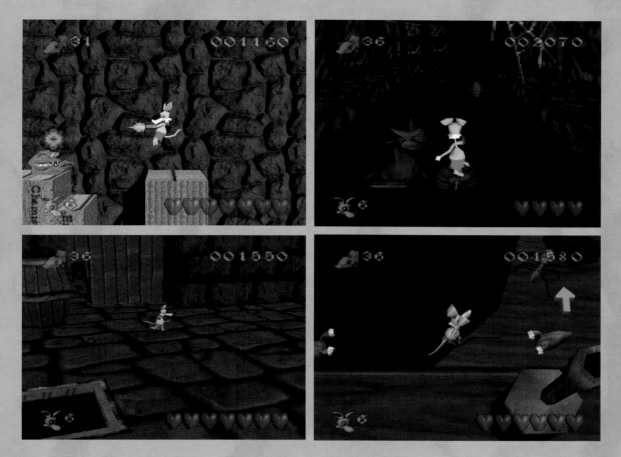

occasional free-roaming segment. It's plagued by terrible controls with some of the heaviest momentum and slowest responses in gaming history, along with the fact that on the first screen, heading up to the first side-scrolling segment throws you into a near thirty-second loading screen, and if you slip off the first ledge, so help you GOD, you get unceremoniously thrown back down to where you came from... after another near thirty-second load screen.

There's also a boss fight known as 'Teapot'. What else could I possibly say? I have provided more information in this small written segment than anyone has done since it first came out in late 1996. By the way, Dazz — for giving me this game so I could make a video about it on my channel? YOU'RE AN ASSHOLE.

# COWBOY BEBOP

**CONSOLE:** SONY PLAYSTATION
**YEAR:** 1998
**DEVELOPER:** BANDAI
**PUBLISHER:** BANDAI
**REGION:** JAPAN

Games adapted from popular anime and manga aren't regularly translated and brought over to the West. When an anime becomes popular in the USA, its games will often be localised, but *Cowboy Bebop* has two games to its name which the West never saw.

*Cowboy Bebop* is an anime that follows a crew of space bounty hunters, who often get themselves into unpredictable situations, leading to some interesting takes on a spacefaring future.

The series' first adaptation into a video game was produced by Bandai, and was released for the original PlayStation in 1998, which is fitting, as the PlayStation makes a cameo appearance in the series. The game allows you to take control of protagonist Spike Spiegel as he flies his spaceship, the *Swordfish II*. The title uses a third-person perspective, and has the player chase down bounties through various levels. Each location is set on-rails, and puts you up against an assortment of enemies along the way, with the player facing a boss at the end of each track before collecting their reward. Bonus points can be spent between stages on upgrading the ship's weapons.

Throughout the game, characters from the show will provide the player with information and tips. The cast are all voiced by their original Japanese voice actors, and the game's soundtrack was even composed by the anime's original composer, Yoko Kanno.

Needless to say, the game was inspired by Nintendo's *Star Fox* series. The title wasn't particularly well received, with many critics citing the game's lack of real flight controls and poor graphics. There's also a total of just six levels, making the game very short. During our play of the game, we also felt it lacked the essence of *Cowboy Bebop*. Throughout the anime, Spike is shown to be foolhardy, but knows when to flee if things get too dangerous. The game pits you against thousands of ships that are eliminated with ease — a situation that wouldn't take place in the anime. Spike never retorts back to his crew during levels, only during cutscenes, making his personality seem lost during gameplay.

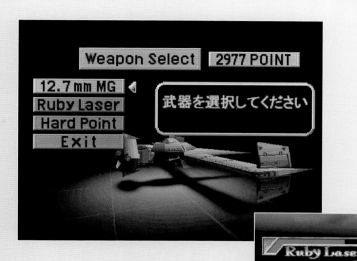

Top two images are from *Cowboy Bebop* on PlayStation 1 game; bottom two images from the *Cowboy Bebop: Serenade of Reminiscence* on PlayStation 2

# COWBOY BEBOP: SERENADE OF REMINISCENCE

**CONSOLE:** SONY PLAYSTATION 2
**YEAR:** 2005
**DEVELOPER:** BANPRESTO
**PUBLISHER:** BANDAI
**REGION:** JAPAN

It would be seven years before another *Cowboy Bebop* game hit the market, once again never leaving Japan. Translated as *Cowboy Bebop: Serenade of Reminiscence*, the next game was created by Bandai subsidiary Banpresto. Released in 2005, it meant the *Cowboy Bebop* world could now be explored as a number of different playable characters in the form of a beat 'em up brawler. The game's developers decided to create an original story exclusively for the title. While the crew are seeking out the overabundance of outlaws with bounties on their heads, the team learn about the existence of a treasure lost by the famous space pirate, Captain H.

The captain would steal from the rich and give to the poor, similar to Robin Hood. Spike and Jet have little interest in the treasure, and think it'll be impossible to find, and so Faye seeks it out on her own. Meanwhile, Spike meets a wanted music producer who tells him of an unpublished pop song by famous singer Priscilla that was lost to the ages. Another of Priscilla's tracks, the fifty-year-old record 'Diamonds', has made a

resurgence in popularity and seems to be played almost everywhere the crew goes. The lost song, titled 'Pearls', is said to be a song to complement 'Diamonds'. Spike decides to seek out the lost song, only to find the track is linked to the lost treasure in its own way.

While Jet is out trying to cash in bounties to fund ship repairs, he encounters the widow

**Matt Barnes:**
Man, I wish they released the PS2 game in the West and dubbed it. I just want more *Cowboy Bebop*, without – of course – making another season. I feel like the games have the perfect opportunity of adding to the TV series by showing the team on random bounties without interfering with the overarching series plot. You can see the potential of this with *Serenade of Reminiscence*; though the game itself is clunky and repetitive a lot is forgiven because it's *Cowboy Bebop*.

of a friend from his policing days at the ISSP. Curious to learn more of his death, Jet decides to investigate the case further. All the while, two rookie bounty hunters, Bianca and Kent, get mixed up with the crew. Faye takes an interest in Kent after learning that he's a descendant of Captain H, as she hopes he'll be able to lead her to the treasure. During their hunt, gangs are out to stop the team from taking their wanted leaders, and another organisation seems eager to find the mysterious treasure before anybody else. Similar to many episodes of *Cowboy Bebop*, there are a number of twists along the way; each of the characters' stories are intertwined, and we're even given more background to the characters.

The game is a mix of several different genres. The game's main focus is on beat 'em up style brawling. The player can combine punches and kicks, and use a range of objects to defeat thugs. Intertwined with these fights are gunplay segments that let the player perform bullet-time-inspired moves. Throughout stages, the player may also need to perform small portions of investigation to find clues, such as hints towards keycodes for locks. A few other gameplay elements are thrown into the mix, such as the player running from danger or piloting a spacecraft. The game also features a stealth-based level and a boat-driving segment. Each style of gameplay was reviewed fairly poorly, with critics citing issues such as lacklustre controls and a reliance on tedious memorisation. One part of the game which was widely praised, however, is the segment where Jet can explore the *Bebop*. This allowed fans to explore the ship seen throughout the anime.

The game manages to portray the overall feeling of the anime series, which is what the original PlayStation 1 title lacked. It stays true to the style of the show, only compromising in a few places to suit the gameplay. Several shots throughout the game also pay homage to the original animation. The soundtrack is mostly comprised of tracks taken from the anime series, though three new tracks were created for the game. These tracks would later appear on the final soundtrack for the series, titled *Cowboy Bebop Tank! THE! BEST!*

## Localisation

The first *Cowboy Bebop* title on the PlayStation 1 was probably never considered for an international release. In 1998, the anime was yet to become a cult hit in America. However, in 2004, reports online stated that *Cowboy Bebop: Serenade of Reminiscence* was set to have an international release. The game was demoed at the Electronic Entertainment Expo (known as E3), and was generally well received. *Bebop* was being regularly aired on Adult Swim in the USA at the time, allowing for the series to garner a massive following. However, in 2004, Bandai updated the game's official English website to change the shipping date from Fall 2004 to Fall 2005, and at the end of 2005, updated it once more to remove the date altogether.

How much of the game was localised before its cancellation remains a mystery. We attempted to contact several voice actors who worked on *Bebop* to see if Bandai ever approached them to work on the game, but received no response. Because the game was set to release in 2005, Bandai might have thought it was a better investment to pursue titles for the upcoming PlayStation 3 than to release games for the soon-to-be-out-of-date PS2. It's also possible that Bandai saw the game's lukewarm critical reception in the West and decided against publishing a product that'd already been labelled as sub-par. This would be unusual however, as the quality of licensed video games is usually quite low.

# CRIME CRACKERS

**CONSOLE:** SONY PLAYSTATION
**YEAR:** 1994
**DEVELOPER:** MEDIA.VISION
**PUBLISHER:** SONY INTERACTIVE
ENTERTAINMENT
**REGION:** JAPAN

# CRIME CRACKERS 2

**CONSOLE:** SONY PLAYSTATION
**YEAR:** 1997
**DEVELOPER:** MEDIA.VISION
**PUBLISHER:** SONY INTERACTIVE
ENTERTAINMENT
**REGION:** JAPAN

Media.Vision had a number of games that were left outside of the US, including the company's first release, *Crime Crackers*. Considered to be pretty popular in its native country, the title even received a sequel: *Crime Crackers 2*.

Out in the vast open nothingness of space, crime is always stirring up in the obsidian sky, almost as infinite as the Universe itself. To combat such crime, an intergalactic organisation known as the Galaxy Police work to put criminals in their place and protect the innocent. However, to help the police with situations that they simply can't handle, the Crime Crackers come in to save the day.

Taking control of the team of crime fighters as they travel the stars in their giant pink dolphin spacecraft, the player will be introduced to some unique and interesting characters. Their captain, Emilia F. Alcanett, dreams of one day rising to the ranks of the Cosmo Guardians, another group of justice enforcers who roam the galaxy. She searches for her brother, who has gone missing.

The game follows a first-person perspective, and in order to attack the player must first enter a battle stance before shooting. The game lends itself more to the dungeon-crawler RPG genre, primarily focusing on exploration. Weapons and armour can be collected throughout the adventure, as well as a variety of items.

The player has control of three different characters at all times, and the character in the middle of the screen takes the lead. This means that they are the one to attack as well as the one to receive damage.

Some consider the game to be playable while not being in English — there is no fan translation available — however it may not be so easy for those who want to complete the title.

The first *Crime Crackers* was a launch title for the PlayStation and was hoped to cause a big impact within the Japanese market. It was not just an early title for Sony's console, but also the first game created by a new

studio. Made in partnership with Sony, Media.Vision didn't see international success until two years later with the release of *Wild Arms*. Having been created in just four months, and having a very Japanese-heavy aesthetic, it's likely Sony felt that it was not worth localising *Crime Crackers* when it was possible it would have had few sales during the early days of the PlayStation launch.

Whilst the game has its issues, such as repetitive dungeons and unpolished mechanics, it did help Media.Vision continue to create more titles with Sony, making some games with wide success.

After Media.Vision's attempt at an alternative RPG received a mixed response, they moved on to create *Rapid Reload*. With their dip into an alternative genre, they went back to their initial skills with RPGs, creating the now highly praised first title in the *Wild Arms* series. A year later, the *Crime Crackers* sequel was released, a more polished game than its

**Dazz:**
*Crime Crackers* is pretty cool, though the gameplay has definitely aged badly. The only real reason I even acknowledged this game during research was because of my love for *Wild Arms*, which is incredibly different. I suppose the main draw for *Crime Crackers* is in the old-school anime aesthetic, with its cool sci-fi vibe. If you can't understand what the characters are saying though, I'd argue it isn't really worth the investment.

predecessor, with many of the earlier issues now fixed.

Whilst a direct continuation, this time the player is put in control of an entirely new cast of characters. The Guppy Team is led by captain Seria Hasselbag, a sixteen-year-old girl who, whilst slightly naive, has a kind heart. Her aspirations are to be as successful in her endeavours as Emilia from the original game, whose team are now known throughout the galaxy as being top-tier bounty hunters.

Seria is joined by Wendy Wilkinson, a blue-haired winged maid; Shiza Kanagusk, a powerful Kenpo specialist; Mardock Hooper, the team's engineer and navigator; and Jonmichael Hasselbag, a droid who acts as a father figure to Seria, sharing her last name. Jonmichael is capable of transforming to a more robust form.

The crew expands as the plot goes on,

providing the player with eight different units to take into battle, more than twice the figure in the first release. With a party of four, the game adds a restoration mechanic that heals fighters who aren't participating in a fight whilst moving around each stage. The player is also now able to look up and down, making aiming more refined.

Several items in the game make reference to earlier Media.Vision games, including Moa Gault, a weapon named after the fire guardian from *Wild Arms*, and Seria's gun 'Rapid Reload'.

## Localisation

With *Crime Crackers 2* (pictured below) being a direct continuation from the first release, publishing this sequel in a region without any following of the series could have been seen as a risky strategy. Sequels that do receive localisation are sometimes rebranded to appear as though they are the first of a series, but with the sequel's plot heavily involving the exploits of the team featured in the first game, this may not have been an easy solution. Their reasoning may also have been that if the company believed the first release wouldn't sell for a variety reasons, what chance would a sequel have?

ただの廃ビルだなんて
ツッコミは、なしにするでヤンス。

# THE DENDY: RUSSIA'S 'OFFICIAL' BOOTLEG NES

The Family Computer, or 'Famicom', was released in 1983 to the Japanese market, with America and Europe getting hold of the hardware in '85 and '86 respectively. Often cited as helping to revitalise the gaming industry in the States, it found its way into the homes of citizens from other countries — though in a different form.

In the early 1990s a Taiwanese company called TXC created and sold the Micro Genius console, a clone of the NES; these consoles were distributed and sold among various countries in which Nintendo had not yet established a market. Working with a company called Steepler, they began creating another 'Famiclone' known as the Dendy. Prior to this console's release, there were few video games available in Russia at all, with personal computers being a rarity themselves.

Victor Savyuk first heard about video game consoles while working for another technology firm, Paragraph. Savyuk says that he knew straight away home consoles had great potential: 'Of course, everybody likes to play games, but in those times, video games were only on computers. They were absolutely not mass market. They were just for freaks, for programming engineers. I immediately understood that this was the future. Thanks to Nintendo and SEGA, and Atari before them, this business existed and it was huge — but it wasn't in Russia. I understood that this was the future, this was a place for new business in Russia.'

Following this, in the summer of 1992, Savyuk approached Steepler with his idea. They responded positively, saying they had already considered something similar. By September of the same year, Victor was head of the division of video games within Steepler, though he was the only employee

**Matt Barnes:**
This is one of the best things we have researched. This Russian rabbit hole kept getting more and more intriguing as we got further in. I highly recommend looking deeper into what is theorised happened to the company Steepler. It's quite an incredible story involving the Federal Agency of Government Communications and Information threatening Steepler, lots of injuries to members of the company, with someone even being run over, and the board of directors eventually abandoning ship and leaving the country for safety. Thrilling!

in the branch. His job was to source the products and prepare them for sale; however, no one at the company knew anything about the video games industry apart from the fact that cloned hardware was being produced in China and Taiwan. With merely a chair, a laptop, phone and fax machine — but no desk — Savyuk began to reach out to companies with a plan to start selling consoles as soon as December 1992. Having never even played a games console before, he faxed designs to a number of companies in order to get sample versions to learn more about aspects of build quality.

Going on erroneous information from a co-worker at Steepler that Russian televisions use PAL-I colour encoding like the UK and other territories, he got a Chinese manufacturer to send over standard PAL-I machines. Unfortunately, on Russian SECAM televisions, the picture would appear in black and white. However, taking this console to an experienced engineer allowed him to find out more about what he actually needed.

Savyuk finally settled for TXC based on their build quality and their competitive prices, as well as the fact that they were one of the few companies that produced video games in the SECAM D/K encoding most prevalent in Russia and Eastern Europe. The console released to weak sales, with SECAM being one of the main issues. The SECAM consoles were more expensive to produce, and as it turned out, the majority of consumers that could afford the console would also tend to buy the newer Japanese televisions that had both SECAM and PAL support. This led to the Dendy only selling 2,000—3,000 units per month at the equivalent of roughly $100 each. It wasn't until six months later that the Dendy Junior was released, featuring the much cheaper PAL encoding. The new console went on sale in June of 1993 and sales almost

immediately exploded, skyrocketing to 70,000–80,000 units being sold per month — roughly twenty-five times more than its predecessor. By August the company had made their first million dollars in a single month. Video-Ace, a publishing house, began the production of the first video-game-focused monthly magazine in August of 1993, *Video-Ace Dendy*. The magazine focused on games being released into the Russian market and would shamelessly use known SEGA and Nintendo brands in their imagery. In order to fill the magazine with content, they borrowed and translated French video game articles from various magazines published by Hachette Filipacchi Presse.

The company struggled financially, and by the sixth issue had officially partnered with Steepler. At the start of the magazine's life, each issue only contained twenty-four pages. After Steepler became involved, it was ultimately extended to a fully fledged magazine of 100 pages including comic strips, rumours, gossip and more fan-centric content. The magazine's name was also eventually changed to *Velikiy Drakon*, meaning 'great dragon'.

A smaller magazine took the moniker of *Video-Ace Dendy*, and was released alongside the original publication. By *Velikiy Drakon*'s eighteenth issue, *Video-Ace Dendy* was cancelled and Steepler pulled its funding.

Steepler started an extensive advertising campaign in 1993 to make more people aware of the Dendy brand. Television commercials were released in December during the build-up to Christmas, with the slogan roughly translating to 'Dendy, Dendy! We all love Dendy! Dendy — everyone plays!' It is thought that Ivan Maximov, the Russian artist and animator who created the brand's mascot, Dendy the Elephant, animated for

these ads. In 1994, *Dendy: The New Reality*, produced by Sorec-Video, aired on TV. The show had a run time of thirty minutes and broadcast on the channel 2x2. The first season lasted thirty-three episodes. In 1995, the second season moved to another channel, ORT, and was produced by Klass! Studio, gradually turning into a weekly clip show until it was cancelled in 1996. The show was hosted by children's television personality Sergei Suponev, presenting the various pirated games that arrived on the Russian scene as if they were official legal Dendy products as well as giving hints and tips. If no new games were available, Sergei would just fill the time by talking to the general public about their thoughts on video games.

In August 1994, Steepler made a joint venture with Incombank to create Dendy as its own business. The newly formed company made a deal with Nintendo in November of 1994, giving the company the exclusive rights to sell the SNES and its games in Russia. This contract extended to *Dendy: The New Reality*, resulting in the show stopping all mention of anything involving SEGA. However, this only lasted two months, and by January of 1995 all mentions of SEGA were back. The mass marketing of the Dendy in Russia had an unusual effect on the brand. People were not only referring to Dendy when talking about video games — it became the noun for video games. This was a problem, as often people couldn't distinguish an official Dendy console from other bootleg consoles. As Steepler offered a one-year warranty with all of their Dendys, ironically they began receiving numerous requests for returns and repairs from consumers who had actually purchased different brands.

The Dendy did feature their own 'officially released' games, though these themselves were bootlegs. There were also countless other bootleg cartridges in circulation from China and Taiwan. The only ways to differentiate between an 'official' cart and another bootleg were the small cardboard sleeve the games came in and a sticker on the back featuring the Dendy elephant and Steepler's phone number. As you would expect, these video game clones led to some pretty bizarre titles, like *Somari*, which is simply a Frankensteined *Sonic* game but with the Sonic sprite being replaced by Mario. Another is *Mario 16*, a clone of *Joe & Mac* but once again featuring Mario. There is a huge assortment of other fake sequels of licensed games, such as *Top Gun 3*, *Tiny Toon Adventures 6* and *Batman Returns 3*, as well as terrible spelling and translations like *Sky Destroter*, *SUP Packmn* and *Hyper Olympic*. The game cartridges were of very low quality when compared to official Nintendo carts. They were prone to cracking and breaking. Not only this but none of the game chips included a battery, meaning that there was no possibility of having save files, which led to the console not featuring a single long-form RPG.

There were also, of course, direct copies of NES games available and often these would be included in the numerous multi-game cartridges, which boast anywhere between 4 and 10 million different games. Though more often than not these cartridges offered repeats of the same games amongst a slew of broken or unplayable clones, some did include more than one actual NES title, meaning that at times, the Russian consumers were buying several games at a fraction of the cost of just one single game in the West.

Having sold more than 1 million consoles already, by the middle of 1994 the Dendy console was selling over 100,000 consoles per month, just two years after its inception. Though Dendy consoles can still be

purchased to this day, there is no link between them and the original Steepler product as Steepler closed its doors in 1996. It is speculated that it was the deal with Nintendo that was the cause of the company's eventual collapse, as the vastly more expensive official Nintendo consoles and cartridges meant the company was incapable of selling them for a profit.

# DOKI DOKI MAJO SHINPAN!

**CONSOLE:** NINTENDO DS
**YEAR:** 2007
**DEVELOPER:** SNK
**PUBLISHER:** SNK
**REGION:** JAPAN

SNK have been developers and publishers since the late 1970s. They have games ranging from the gorgeously illustrated *Metal Slug* to the widely played fighting series *King of Fighters*. But when it comes to games under their belt which we never saw, there is one series that stands out as being very risqué. That series is *Doki Doki Majo Shinpan!*, which means 'Heart-Pounding Magical Investigation'.

The first game in the series was released in 2007, and sees the player take on the role of Akuji Nishimura, a junior high school student who has been tasked by an angel, known as LuLu, to locate a witch that has managed to infiltrate the school undetected. The reason he accepts this mission is because Akuji is proud of his status as a 'bad boy', and LuLu has threatened him with the possibility of being turned into a 'good boy' if he fails. The only way of finding a witch in this universe is to discover a mark on their body, known as the 'witch mark'. This is where it becomes fairly obvious as to why this game was never released internationally.

The player must talk to the various students and characters that they encounter in a visual novel type environment before taking part in battles with the characters. This will soon progress further when the player has to probe the character by touching their body and looking for the witch mark.

While the game had several promotional websites — not only in Japanese, but also English, Chinese and Korean — these soon disappeared after a sequel was confirmed to be in production, and the Japanese site was changed to try and promote the next instalment. When gaming gossip site Kotaku asked if the game would receive a release in the United States, an SNK spokesperson responded, 'This title is only for the Japanese market. We do not have any plans to localise the other versions.'

The game proved to be popular prior to its release in Japan, with Amazon claiming that the title had the best pre-order figures in the region, attaining higher demand than the then upcoming first-party Nintendo title *The Legend of*

*Zelda: Phantom Hourglass*. However, this demand didn't stick, and the game only attained a total of 50,000 sales. Reception was generally negative, with worries that the content of the title was creepy and involved situations that people should feel uncomfortable in. This is likely because of the game's large cast of girls with varying backgrounds and ages.

The game's characters include:

Maho Akai, a fourteen-year-old cheerleader with pink hair and a large bust.

Maria Abe, a fourteen-year-old fortune teller who follows the meganekko archetype of a young character considered to be attractive for wearing glasses.

Yuuma Mochizuki, a thirteen-year-old boy who takes everything too seriously and is constantly getting himself hurt.

Renge Oda, a thirteen-year-old gamer who adores her NES copy of *Athena*, a game created by SNK in the 1980s.

Merry Watabiki, a twelve-year-old girl who can be seen almost always wearing a rabbit costume.

Ayame Midoh, a fifteen-year-old only child and daughter of a Shinto shrine priest and priestess.

Eve Seiya, the school's twenty-three-year-old nurse.

And lastly, Noel Seiya, Eve's sister who also happens to be an archangel.

While most of these ages seem very low to people from the West, the age of consent in Japan is actually thirteen. That means these characters are of legal age, and the actions conducted within the game fall within the law; however, this may not be the case with Merry Watabiki, who is only twelve years of age. With that said, she has the least risqué elements found within the game.

However, the game's lack of sales didn't stop SNK from creating a sequel a year later, titled *Doki Doki Majo Shinpan 2 Duo*. The sequel follows the same gameplay as the first, though it now includes a more extensive touch mode and also makes use of the DS microphone. This time around the game also received a CERO rating of D, for ages seventeen and up, while the first game only had a CERO rating of C, for ages fifteen and up.*

While the game's plot follows Akuji once again, the suspects have changed. Characters now include:

* The Computer Entertainment Rating Organization of Japan.

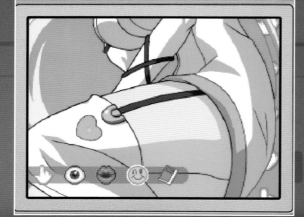

in typical goth Lolita clothing.

Rekka Nagisa, a skilled sword wielder with red hair.

Sophy Hiro, the school's maid, whose name is based on a play of the Japanese word for 'philosophy'.

Sales were worse than ever before with the sequel, attaining only 30,000 sales in total. To put this in context, *The Legend of Zelda: Phantom Hourglass* was released the same year, on the same platform and sold just under 1 million copies in Japan; this was considered a success. Surprisingly, a year later and only two years after its release, the first game received an enhanced release called *Doki Majo Plus*. Often referred to as a third title in the series, the game retells the events of the first release with a revised soundtrack and introduces a single new character, Kiara Natsuminami.

The series had even more of a push into the market with a manga based on the games being produced.

## Localisation

The games likely never had the translation treatment after Western reviewers made claims that the game was one that should be avoided at all costs with its controversial content. The reason that SNK had no intention of releasing the game internationally is probably due to the young age of many of the game's cast. SNK would have had a lot of work on their hands making the games sell well after knowing that they had already sold poorly to Japanese audiences, and with a high age rating being guaranteed, the cartoony artwork would not have been so well received by the Western market.

Himeki Sakura, a reporter for the school magazine who keeps her camera with her at all times.

Kamome Tomozato, a girl with an extreme passion for comics and anime. She has a penchant for ninjas and ninja-related games.

Koron Seihana, a troublemaker friend of Akuji who dreams of one day becoming a pastry chef.

Kureha Haori, a popular student who attains high grades with her own fan club.

Nagi and Nami Futaba, athletic twin swimmers with a friendly rivalry.

Neon Rizumi, a fashion idol who dresses

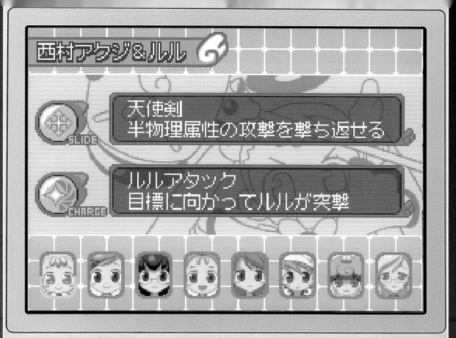

西村アクジ&ルル

SLIDE
天使剣
半物理属性の攻撃を撃ち返せる

CHARGE
ルルアタック
目標に向かってルルが突撃

MIC.

# DOOR DOOR

**CONSOLE:** NINTENDO FAMICOM AND PC-8801
**YEAR:** 1985
**DEVELOPER:** CHUNSOFT
**PUBLISHER:** ENIX
**REGION:** JAPAN

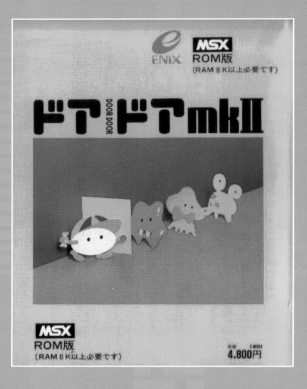

Many gamers know of Enix, publisher of several popular RPGs in the mid-nineties. Their growth and strong presence in the gaming world led to a merger with Squaresoft to form Square-Enix. Both companies were known for RPGs, creating some of the genre's bestselling games. However, Enix's first published title was little more than a puzzle game that never reached America. That game is *Door Door*.

*Door Door* sees players controlling the character Chun, a small ball-like white creature that wears a baseball cap. The aim of the game is to capture aliens by trapping them behind doors throughout each stage. To capture the aliens, the player must first open a door, and when an alien walks in, they must close the door behind them. Once closed, a door cannot be reopened. If the player leaves a door open for too long after an alien enters, it can escape, and will need to be recaptured.

Bonus items appear when aliens are locked away, and higher scoring items spawn for capturing multiple aliens at the same time. To capture multiple aliens at once, the player must figure out each alien's mannerisms. Some aliens follow Chun in a direct path, some take a roundabout route using ladders, while others mimic the player's jumps. Chun can only walk, climb ladders and perform a small jump. Since the player has few techniques at their disposal, avoiding the aliens can be a real struggle. As the game progresses, other

hazards appear, such as nails on the ground or slides the player can fall down. New ladder types are also introduced that either only aliens or Chun can use.

As a result, the player can come up with creative strategies for capturing multiple aliens by dying on purpose. Closed doors will reopen when the player dies, but the aliens trapped behind them won't respawn. The player must take note of how many doors and enemies are in a level and where they're placed. For example, two enemies appear in Level 10, but there's only one door. Both aliens are initially too far apart to be captured in quick succession without one escaping. To trap them, the player must manoeuvre both aliens closer together. If the player only captures one alien, they're forced into a no-win scenario and must sacrifice a life to progress.

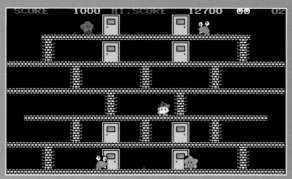

**NEC PC-8801**

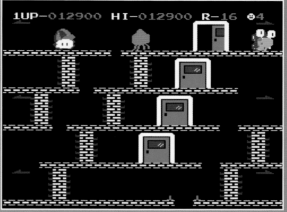

**Famicom**

The game's origins are perhaps its most interesting talking point. Yasuhiro Fukushima renamed his company Enix in 1982 after being inspired by the personal computer industry forming in the United States. Although he wasn't a programmer, Fukushima wanted Enix to be a company that could publish titles created by other talented individuals in the field. To find that talent, the company set up a national programming contest which garnered 300 entries. First prize went to the creator of *Door Door*, Koichi Nakamura. The year after the game's release, Nakamura founded the game development company Chunsoft, named after Chun from *Door Door*. The company merged with game developer Spike in 2012 and is now known as Spike Chunsoft. Koichi Nakamura was hired by Enix, and all rights to *Door Door* became Enix's property. Enix published *Door Door* on several Japanese home computers in 1983, and with sales exceeding 200,000 copies.

Another noteworthy person, Yuji Horii, was hired as result of the contest after making it to the finals with a tennis game. One of Enix's next releases, a game by Horii called *The Portopia Serial Murder Case*, is credited as the reason *Metal Gear* creator Hideo Kojima entered the video game industry.

This game was originally published on the more obscure NEC PC-8801, but as the console market grew bigger within the industry, a Famicom version of *Door Door* was published in 1985. A year later, the company created the RPG that would make Horii and Nakamura prominent names in the industry: *Dragon Quest*. Horii later worked as supervisor for the Super Nintendo RPG *Chrono Trigger*, and even made a cameo appearance in the title.

## Localisation

*Door Door* falls into a common category of game at the time. It was a random puzzle game that wasn't anything revolutionary or groundbreaking — it was just a puzzle game. The reason America never saw it was probably because the companies involved in its creation weren't big enough to warrant funding an international venture. That said, the game is notable in Japan. Famitsu editors even put the title among the likes of *Super Mario Bros.* and *Donkey Kong* on their list of the best Famicom games ever released.

# E.X. TROOPERS

**CONSOLE:** SONY PLAYSTATION 3, NINTENDO 3DS
**YEAR:** 2012
**DEVELOPER:** CAPCOM (3DS, PS3), HEXADRIVE (PS3)
**PUBLISHER:** CAPCOM
**REGION:** JAPAN

It's not rare to see a spinoff for a popular series fail to receive international localisation. The resulting game can often be something new and interesting, providing a fresh look at a series fans already know and love. The *Lost Planet* series had three releases in the West, each being a third-person shooter in which the player must fight off aliens while inhabiting a planet known as E.D.N. III, which is currently going through an ice age. Prior to the release of *Lost Planet 3*, Capcom released a Japan exclusive title for the series which deviated from the typical style of the previous two titles. This entry into *Lost Planet* is called *E.X. Troopers*.

E.X. Troopers was released in 2012 for both Nintendo 3DS and the PlayStation 3. It was developed and published by Capcom, with help from Hexadrive for the PlayStation 3 release. Deviating dramatically from the presentation style that fans had known from *Lost Planet*, Capcom describes *E.X. Troopers* as having 'exhilarating manga-esque action' in contrast to the action or cinematic shooting presentation from the other entries to the series.

The game plays similarly to previous *Lost Planet* titles, with gameplay seeing the player navigate through stages of extreme icy landscapes from a third-person perspective. The player can equip two weapons prior to each mission, typically a

lighter weapon with high ammo capacity and a stronger weapon with limited ammunition. Each weapon's ammo will regenerate after a short cooldown.

The player is also capable of boosting and dodging, to allow for more action-based combat. By utilising both boosts and melee attacks, combined with projectile attacks, the player must complete a variety of goals for missions. These range from defending or enabling points, to simply killing all enemies within a stage.

By completing missions, the player obtains experience to level up and improve their character as well as currency to help improve weapons or armour. These upgrades require that the player has a number of materials too, which are collected throughout missions or by speaking with various NPCs in the game's hub maps. Medals are awarded for each goal that has been achieved within a mission, with special VR missions having more goals than standard missions during a first run of the game. Medals can be spent to buy music tracks and costumes for characters. Costumes can also be unlocked through the use of codes, allowing the player to unlock costumes with ties to various different manga and Capcom game series.

The game's plot follows Bren, a candidate for the Neo Venus Construction (NEVEC) educational facility located on E.D.N. III. While being transported to the institution on a spacecraft, the transport fleet of new recruits is attacked by a number of unknown Vital Suit mechs. Bren is selected by educational instructor Walter Stringray to assist him in piloting a prototype Vital Suit loaded with a next-generation AI able to operate with full automation. As the suit's new master, Bren names the machine Gingira and works with Walter to bring the enemy units down.

After successfully taking out the enemies, Bren and Walter have no choice but to make an emergency ejection from Gingira while entering the atmosphere of E.D.N. III. This is where Bren discovers the planet's harsh surroundings and encounters the alien race known as the Akrid. From a base of operations acting as a sort of school, the team take on missions and fight back against the Akrid.

## Localisation

The reason for the game's lack of localisation is of particular interest, as while Capcom had initially filed for a trademark on the name *E.X. Troopers* in 2011 for the US and European markets, when asked about a potential Western release, senior VP of Capcom, Christian Svensson, stated on Capcom's 'Ask Capcom' forum: 'Guys, I have no news to share on that front right now. Sorry.'

Moments later he also stated that '*E.X. Troopers* isn't part of the LP series officially (thus the difference in name), nor are there plans to bring it westward at this time.'

It's possible that plans might have changed with a successful release to the Japanese market, but upon release, the 3DS sold 17,000 copies and the PlayStation 3 only 8,700. These sales figures make the game the weakest debut sales for any game within the *Lost Planet* series, possibly because the game was competing for sales against *Call of Duty: Black Ops II* which was released around the same time.

The game has a strong Japanese theme to it, with the game's style following the manga and anime aesthetic very closely. It's possible that Capcom believed this change in direction for a series considered to be quite serious in the West would be unsuccessful. The game is rather dialogue heavy, with long cutscenes featuring full voice acting, meaning that the cost of localising the game could outweigh the likelihood of strong sales.

| CONSOLE: | SONY PLAYSTATION 2, SEGA DREAMCAST AND PC |
| YEAR: | 2001 |
| DEVELOPER: | IN UTERO, UBISOFT |
| PUBLISHER: | UBISOFT (PS2), BIGBEN INTERACTIVE (DREAMCAST), MICROSOFT (PC), 1C COMPANY |
| REGION: | EUROPE |

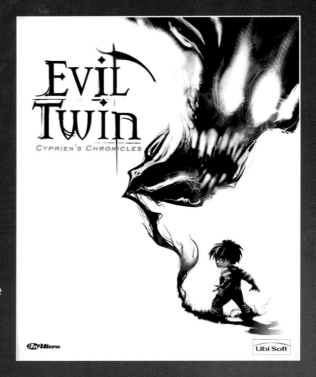

Platformer titles released around the turn of the millennium were no rare sight, with several of the most critically acclaimed games within the genre releasing towards the late nineties. This next generation of platformers expanded their traditional audience, encompassing darker themes. One of the lesser known games released back in 2001 was the PAL-exclusive *Evil Twin: Cyprien's Chronicles*.

*Evil Twin* was developed by In Utero and published by Ubisoft on the PlayStation 2 and Windows, as well as being published by Bigben Interactive on the SEGA Dreamcast. The game plays like any standard 3D platformer, with inspirations from the likes of German Expressionism movement in film. It follows the story of a young orphan named Cyprien, starting out on his birthday, where he is joined by his friends Dave, Joey, Vince and Steve.

Cyprien's reaction to his party is morose and detached, justified by his past.

Greg:
Growing up in merry ol' England (well 'ello me ol' mucka toodlepipwhatsittoya), we had the good fortune of actually getting to play this gem when it first came out. I was dubious about going back to revisit it for fear that a replay could tarnish my fond memories. It was in fact the opposite: I was pleasantly surprised at how well this game has held up. The characters and the world they're in are imaginative and compelling, and the 3D platforming still has the same satisfying steadiness that I remembered. The game is of course not without its flaws. Just as an example, the first-person aiming is sloppy (see *Ocarina of Time* for further details) but things like this are only minor niggles in a great game and I would highly recommend checking it out if you get the chance.

Cyprien's presence within the orphanage comes from his parents dying on his birthday, leaving him to feel alone in the world. After returning to his room in a state of depression, Cyprien is greeted by his teddy bear Lenny, who has been given life through Cyprien's imagination. Becoming increasingly aggravated by the barrage of questions he's receiving, Cyprien becomes overwrought with dark, vehement thoughts, striking back at Lenny by reminding him that he is nothing but a toy, before condemning his world of Undabed to oblivion.

Little does Cyprien know that by giving in to sinister thoughts, a darkness has swept over the orphanage, causing Lenny to disappear while shadows emerge to take his friends. Regaining consciousness, Cyprien finds himself alone in the world of Undabed. Here he meets Wilbur, a friend of Lenny's. Wilbur explains that the world he's inhabiting didn't always appear this way. It was once a world not dissimilar to Cyprien's, before a wave swept it all away and a tower appeared known as Loren Darith. At this time, a being known as the Master took control of the world, and the people became powerless against his armies.

The Master then manipulated the people of the world by erasing traces of the past and entrusting a key known as the Great Zippete to the citizens of Demi Island. In an attempt to take back control, Lenny sought out the key, but was arrested before he was able to complete his mission. The Master then split the key into four pieces and spread it across the world of Undabed, and now it's up to Cyprien to free Lenny by obtaining all four parts of the Great Zippete.

He soon discovers that the islands that survived the wave of darkness are ruled over by evil incarnations of his real-world friends from his orphanage.

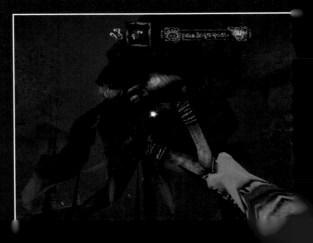

VMU

The game plays like most standard third-person platform titles, with the player able to manoeuvre and jump around the stage. To attack enemies, the player can make use of a slingshot. It's also possible to enter a first-person view where the player is able to make more precise shots or activate switches.

The world is filled with a variety of collectable items, including basic health pickups, as well as items to fill the player's SuperCyp gauge. By filling this bar, it's possible to transform into Cyprien's imaginary superhero state, SuperCyp, a character that he created while playing with his friends in the real world. SuperCyp is capable of firing long-range fireball attacks, causing more damage than his standard slingshot. The game's first publication was on the PlayStation 2 in 2001, but was intended for release two years prior. This initial planned release was simply titled *Evil Twin*, and before that the story was conceived as an animated series. Julie Salzmann, the game's marketing manager, stated:

'To start with, *Evil Twin* was intended for television, with a series of animated films whose theme explored childhood fears in a harrowing and distorted atmosphere. Faced with the magnitude of the project and the technical skills involved, and thanks to the advice of a TV producer, we turned toward the game medium.'

Through a long stage of planning and creation, the game's Dreamcast publication came in 2002, and it was one of the final games published on the platform.

In early previews of the game found in *NextGen* magazine, it was revealed that the title would boast special features in this Dreamcast release. This included

downloadable costumes, as well as four VMU minigames. While never making it into the final release, these minigames were published online after the fact by Omar Cornut, the developer of these minigames. He stated that due to complications with development, they were left out from the game's retail launch.

These games include *Paper Attack*, *Swampy*, *Fat Rain* and *Glucky Labyrinth*.

*Paper Attack* is a simple arcade-style shooter. *Swampy* is a puzzle game in which the player must navigate a frog on a set of lily pads, touching each pad once and only once. *Fat Rain* requires the player to throw a ball at an enemy who is constantly vomiting food which must be caught. And *Glucky Labyrinth* is a labyrinth navigation game using a 3D view, though it was never finished.

## Localisation

It's possible that complications in development led to delays, causing the team to fall back on their plans to release the title outside of PAL markets. The poor sales this caused left the studio in financial difficulties and due to delays, the Dreamcast release was handled by Bigben Interactive, a firm known for being one of the last to publish titles for the system in Europe after the console was discontinued. Reviews praised the game's overall art direction and the musical compositions of Bertrand Eluerd, but it was slated for its poor controls. In Utero, a Canadian development studio, only ever released a few games, with *Evil Twin* being one of their last.

*Well, gulp, I mean to shay, it keepth me busy. Some people do knitting, I make nets.*

# FATAL FRAME: MASK OF THE LUNAR ECLIPSE

**CONSOLE:** NINTENDO WII
**YEAR:** 2008
**DEVELOPER:** NINTENDO SOFTWARE
PLANNING & DEVELOPMENT,
TECMO, GRASSHOPPER
MANUFACTURE
**PUBLISHER:** NINTENDO
**REGION:** JAPAN

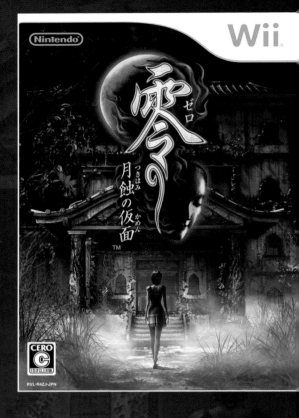

The Japanese are often seen as the founding fathers for many popular genres of game, perhaps none more so than horror. America saw most entries in the *Fatal Frame* series, or as it's known in Europe, the *Project Zero* series. Two games remained overseas, however. One of these was a remake of the second *Fatal Frame* for the Wii, but we'll be looking at the other: the fourth entry in the series, *Fatal Frame: Mask of the Lunar Eclipse*.

*Fatal Frame: Mask of the Lunar Eclipse* was released exclusively to Japanese audiences in 2008 for the Nintendo Wii and marked the series' first venture onto Nintendo hardware. All prior games were only released for PlayStation 2 and Xbox. *Mask of the Lunar Eclipse* was actually published by Nintendo themselves, and

they were partially involved in the game's development process alongside Grasshopper Manufacture, while lead development was handled by series creators Tecmo.

**Matt Barnes:**
We owe a lot to Gab Smolders with this trivia, having not played through the *Fatal Frame* series ourselves; it was tough dissecting a horror sequel that was all in Japanese. So it helped that she is fluent in the language, especially when it came to understanding the weird narrative. Definitely check out her channel for all things horror; she does a lot of Let's Plays of some awesome scary region-locked games.

To ensure that each game could act as a standalone entry in the series, the team decided against having a numerical indicator for each title. While there are consistent elements that tie the games together, they can be played individually as self-contained stories.

Chronologically, *Mask of the Lunar Eclipse* is the first entry in the series timeline.

The year is 1980, six years prior to Miku Hinasaki entering the Himuro Mansion in the first *Fatal Frame* release. Of a group of five friends, two of the girls have passed away under inexplicable circumstances. Of the remaining survivors, Misaki Asou and Madoka Tsukimori return to the island they grew up on, hoping to solve the mystery surrounding their friends' demise. After not hearing back from Misaki and Madoka, Ruka, the third survivor and the game's main protagonist, decides to follow suit.

What ties these girls together is that they know they were kidnapped on the island ten years earlier, but strangely they have no memories of the place other than that they were found together, unharmed, and were taken off the island.

It isn't long before Madoka is killed by angered spirits and Kirishima appears, responding to Ruka's mother's request to help her while on the island.

The Hidden Moon Disease, also known as the Luna Sedata Syndrome, has spread across Rougetsu Island. Patients suffering

from this affliction slowly lose their memories, eventually leading to confusion and paranoia. The disease got its name because one of the side effects was patients seeking out the moon. Seeing the moon or standing in its light would calm them down, and they seemed to temporarily reach clarity. They would be scared of any reflective surface, because they weren't able to recognise their own face, claiming that it looked blurred or distorted. The disease can be transferred just by sight: you only have to witness the face of someone in the later stages of the Hidden Moon Disease to contract it yourself.

The Camera Obscura is an invention by Dr Kunihiko Asou. Searching ways to get closer to the afterlife, Asou invented several devices that could capture supernatural phenomena, like a camera and a spirit radio. Throughout his life, Asou continued improving his camera technology and left it behind in places he thought that it could be of use someday, like the hotel he was staying at while on Rougetsu Island. The camera was later gifted to the local Asou museum, where it is picked up in 1980 by Madoka and later Ruka.

Several film types can be loaded into the camera, which have different levels of power. The higher the power of the film, the more effective it will be in capturing ghosts. Type-Zero film, however, is its own class, and the most powerful. Some of *Fatal*

http://www.nintendo.co.jp

零
月蝕の仮面

*Frame*'s final bosses can only be hurt by this rare type of film. The camera can also be upgraded to, for example, capture a wider angle, or take more powerful shots. Filters and lenses can also be applied for bonus damage or other attributes. These upgrades can be purchased with crystals found throughout the game or points accumulated through fighting ghosts. Points can also be used to unlock additional outfits.

The fourth *Fatal Frame* was the first game to include a new weapon, the Spirit Stone Flashlight. Developed by Dr Asou, it supposedly contains a spirit stone as the name would suggest, giving it the power to exorcise ghosts with a concentrated blast of light. Lenses can also be applied for extra power or other functions.

Development for *Mask of the Lunar Eclipse* was split across three studios, with Tecmo taking charge of gameplay and

atmosphere, while Grasshopper Manufacture took control of the game's character animations and a variety of other elements. Nintendo was also involved, managing general production of the title.

The game was initially conceived when series co-creator Keisuke Kikuchi first took notice of Wii hardware. He, alongside the other series co-creator, Makoto Shibata, took on the roles of producer and director respectively, while also bringing in Goichi Suda, known as Suda51, to help co-direct, co-write and design the title. Suda was initially unsure about working on the project because of his distaste towards horror titles and ghosts in particular.

The *Fatal Frame* series was created with the intention of making a scary title for a wider Japanese audience, leading the team to move away from monsters or zombies, which they felt geared more toward a Western audience, choosing to feature

## Localisation

With such an iconic set of developers attac
to the title, it was surprising to many that
there was a lack of localisation internationa
after all prior releases in the series made t
way overseas. Fans of the series made the
displeasure at this quite apparent: Nintend
America president, Reggie Fils-Aimé, claim
in an interview with MTV at the time, 'We a
not the publisher of that title in the Americ
Not long after, this was followed by an offic
statement from Tecmo:

'Nintendo holds the publishing rights
*Fatal Frame* Wii, which was developed b
Tecmo Ltd. and Grasshopper Manufactu
and released in Japan on 31 July, 2008.
Nintendo of America has since then
decided not to publish the title in North
America — consequently, the title will no
be released in this territory. As the owne
of the IP, Tecmo feels very unfortunate t
the fans of the series in North America
will not have a chance to play the game,
but respects the final decision made by
Nintendo of America.'

Rumours circulated online that the act
reason was because of a dispute betweer
Nintendo and Tecmo. Allegedly, Nintendo
requested that Tecmo make alterations to
the game for a Western release in order t
fix a number of bugs, as well as the game
often criticised controls, which Tecmo had
apparently refused to do. Whether this is
true has not been confirmed.

Adding to the confusion, online reports
indicated that the game was set for a
European release. The game received sto
page listings on European websites, and
popular localisation company XSEED spo
on the matter of a US release. When aske
they would be localising the game, execu
VP Ken Berry stated,

'If you're talking about *Fatal Frame 4*

ghosts instead. With *Mask of the Lunar
Eclipse*, the team chose to base the game
on a desolate island in the 1980s to have the
characters seem truly alone, with cell phones
having not yet become commonplace.

Makoto Shibata and Keisuke Kikuchi were
interviewed by Nintendo for the game's
release. Shibata spoke about how the duo
were excited to be working with a large
selection of developers, as they felt it would
make everybody work harder to create a
great game. They accredited Nintendo for
keeping them on their toes, making sure
the story had no vague plot holes, and
telling them when they thought it wasn't
scary enough.

A selection of Easter eggs are also
found in the game courtesy of Nintendo's
attachment. After completing the game, the
player unlocks two new outfits: Zero Suit
Samus from the *Metroid* series, and Luigi, à

even though it won't be by us. Can't tell you who's bringing it over, but keep your eyes peeled for an official announcement, hopefully sometime soon.' There were even paid-for advertisements in *Official Nintendo Magazine* for both France and Spain in April 2009 claiming that the game 'Will Haunt Your Wii Next Month', suggesting a proposed release in May of 2009.

One thing's for certain though, the game ultimately did not see any international release. As a result, fans of the game created their own translation patch in January 2010. This required files to be stored on a user's SD card or USB hard drive. Making sure to not contribute to piracy of the game, the team ensured that an official retail copy must be present in the disc drive in order to execute the patch which would also bypass the console's region locking. At the time, homebrew on the Wii console was in its infancy.[*] Through the use of an exploit of the console's SD card menu, the translation worked before any semblance of a homebrew channel existed. Since then, the translation can now simply be launched through homebrew applications.

---

[*]   Homebrew games are created without licence or authorisation from the console manufacturer; they are most commonly made by independent developers.

# THE FIREMEN

**CONSOLE:** NINTENDO SUPER FAMICOM,
SUPER NINTENDO
ENTERTAINMENT SYSTEM
**YEAR:** 1994
**DEVELOPER:** HUMAN ENTERTAINMENT
**PUBLISHER:** HUMAN ENTERTAINMENT
**REGION:** JAPAN, EUROPE

The emergency-service career isn't one that has been ignored as games have made their way into popular culture. The idea of seeing a police officer taking a starring role is no new thing, similarly so for games based on doctors and nurses. But one emergency service put in place for the safety of the public which has been largely ignored is that of a firefighter. There are but a few games that cover the role, with one of the first fully fledged commercial titles being exclusive to the Japanese and European regions. That game is *The Firemen* on the SNES.

*The Firemen* was created by Human Entertainment and released in 1994. Set in 2010 but released in the nineties, the game takes a modest look at how the future could have been. Technology has advanced only slightly, and so a basic firefighting squad is still the standard way of handling fires. On the evening of a Christmas party being held for staff at a chemical development company known as Microtech, a fire has broken out and is rapidly spreading across the building. With no other options for a safe mission to be carried out, it's up to the unit to extinguish the fire at any cost and rescue stranded civilians lost throughout the complex.

Due to the abundant supply of chemicals, the fire has spread at an alarming rate across the high rise. The city's D-sector fire brigade has dispatched a unit, formed of Pete, Daniel,

Max, Walter and Winona. After arriving on the scene, the team learns of a large supply of the chemical MDL within the building's basement, known to explode when introduced to excessive heat. The unit splits up in order to obtain the MDL as quickly as possible, in hopes of delivering it to the roof in order blow up a water tank which should help to extinguish the blaze.

The player takes control of Pete Grey and Daniel McClean's operation within the mission, two members of the unit who have twice received commendations for their bravery. Pete is the captain of the five-member unit, while Daniel is his second in command. Daniel is able to take care of himself, making use of his fire axe and lighter load to operate control panels and open doors throughout the duo's ascent. Pete has a water hose at his disposal with an infinitely abundant supply of water. He's able to use this high-powered hose to fire water in any direction around him from great distance, while also using it to extinguish flames that might be rising from below him.

While Pete is projecting water in any direction, the player can hold in a shoulder button in order for him to remain facing in the direction of a flame while moving around. The team can also make use of handheld grenades which release water with a moderate blast radius, though these are limited and must be found throughout the building.

By finding civilians, Pete will be able to restore a portion of his health, and at the end of each stage, the two must extinguish an extremely dangerous flame in the form of a boss battle. Due to the advanced nature of the work carried out in the building, flames don't just appear as simple fires that must be extinguished but instead various hazards that can take the player out. Ceilings that fall in, robots that have been fully engulfed in flames, or flames with aggressive habits and patterns will also become more common as the two proceed further through the building.

The game is made up of stages with a time limit, and while the player has unlimited ammunition, lives are limited to only three continues. Daniel is fully controlled by the game's AI and, being invincible, is a much-needed partner. However, as progress is made through Microtech's laboratories, backdraught becomes more and more common, and thus opening doors could result in huge explosions which will damage the player if they are within the blast radius.

## Localisation

While the game's setting is in New York, featuring a firefighting team of Americans, the game never saw release in America. It did receive a full translation and was ultimately localised for Europe, however, featuring English, French and German languages. The game's lack of localisation within the US is interesting, as one could assume that the game's region-locked status is due to the theme of firefighters being considered uninteresting to the American audience; however, *The Ignition Factor* from Jaleco did receive a release in the States.

While an alleged prototype for a version of the game set to be released in the US surfaced online, one of the owners of a prototype cart, Evan G, performed research only to come to the conclusion that the prototypes were likely only early PAL localisations which had not been script-checked yet. Coverage of the title within America can be found in *Electronic Gaming Monthly* issues of August and September in 1994, where it was first covered in a small segment on Japanese games, later receiving a double-page spread but still not stating any plans for a localisation.

The series proved popular enough within the Japanese market that a sequel was created for the PlayStation, this time published only within Japan. The game featured a two-player option and added voice acting, but is considered to be a step backwards for the game's action.

Human Entertainment stopped operations towards the end of the nineties, leaving a number of franchises to disappear with it. The company's most notable series, *Fire Pro Wrestling*, continued on beyond the development house's demise with Spike, and the only other title that had much of an impact in the West was *Clock Tower*, but with the progression of the survival horror genre at the time, not many people took much notice of Human Entertainment's disappearance. *The Firemen* and its sequel comprise a set of two games which remained within obscurity and stayed with Human Entertainment to the bitter end.

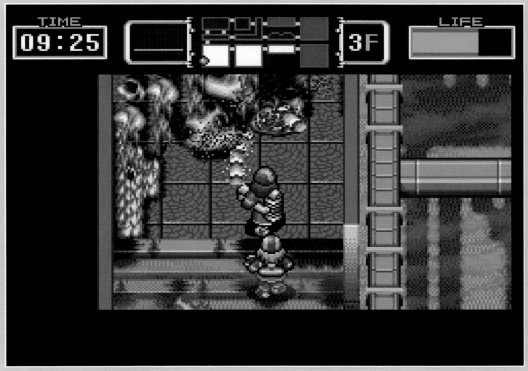

| GUEST: | ASHENS |
| CONSOLE: | ZX SPECTRUM |
| YEAR: | 1984 |
| DEVELOPER: | LEGEND |
| PUBLISHER: | LEGEND |
| REGION: | EUROPE |

Legend made a name for themselves in the UK Spectrum games scene with their very first release in 1983: the excellent RPG *Valhalla*, based on Norse mythology. Amazing for the time, you typed in text commands and little animated stick figures on the screen carried them out. With a sense of humour and fun, *Valhalla* was a smash hit and gamers were excited for Legend's next release. Their follow-up was *The Great Space Race*, a heavily advertised release packaged in a big plastic box with a poster and hefty instruction manual. Sadly for the many people eagerly awaiting its release, the game itself was considerably less impressive.

An attempt at a strategy management game crossed with a graphic adventure, *The Great Space Race* tasks you with supplying some kind of super space booze to ninety-six different space stations across the galaxy. You need to hire four different 'racer' characters, each of which has their own spaceship and rudimentary personality. You then arm their ships and send them off to try and deliver the amazing alcohol before your opponents do.

To say the gameplay is lacking would be a severe understatement. The game pretty much plays itself and just asks you a question every so often that requires a multiple-choice answer. You have a few seconds to choose and if you don't press anything it makes its own decision. And even if you do make a choice, there's a chance your racer will ignore you and choose another option anyway!

For example, one of the small handful of scenarios involves a racer coming across a booby-trapped space wreck. You have to pick from a set of numerical codes and if you choose the wrong one the racer's ship is destroyed. There is no way to determine the correct one — you just have to pick randomly and hope for the best. What fun!

The graphics are a very mixed bag. Much pre-release hype centred around a unique system for animating the racer's faces, but whilst they're well drawn, they actually barely move at all — just an occasional mouth or eye movement. The rest of the graphics are awful, with nearly everything made up of ugly blocks. The space battles (which you have no control over whatsoever) are particularly poor, with tiny, appallingly drawn ships flickering around the screen while some lines flash. Sound barely exists, consisting entirely of a few clicks, beeps and shrieks. Technically the whole game is cripplingly slow, and so unresponsive that you have to hold a button down for seconds before t even registers. Considering you only have about six seconds to make a decision it really doesn't help proceedings.

But the real crime of *The Great Space Race* is that it's crushingly dull. It asks you the same few questions over and over again, the majority of which just require a yes or no answer, and that's the entirety of the game. It's supposed to be a grand space opera but all you do is occasionally decide if you should sober up one of your racers who has drunk too much space booze. (Astonishingly you do this by spending more booze, which also doubles as currency.) It's great that Legend tried to do something weird and unique, but sadly they couldn't get their game to keep up with their ideas, and the result is a tedious, empty bag of nothing. As an employee of Legend told *Sinclair User* magazine, 'The programmers weren't up to it.'

The game was understandably savaged by the press at the time, particularly as it cost a hefty £15 — the equivalent of about £45 in today's money. It received an average of 37% across reviews from the major magazines of the time, and later appeared in several 'worst game of the year' style articles. It also crippled Legend, who reportedly spent £250,000 on it — an insane amount of money for a game at the time. They bailed out distributors who had masses of unsold copies, and even offered their next game (the far superior *Komplex*) half price to disappointed buyers. The company sadly collapsed just before releasing the sequel *Komplex City*, which was apparently complete and of very high quality.

*The Great Space Race* is a real curiosity. An ambitious attempt to make something that had never been seen before, it ultimately failed on all levels. But it certainly wasn't the last space trading simulator — less than a year later Firebird Software released the seminal *Elite*, one of the most highly regarded games of the 8-bit era that lives on to this day as *Elite Dangerous*.

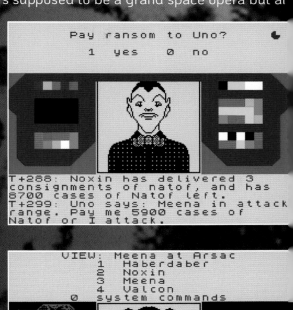

# GUNPLE: GUNMAN'S PROOF

| | |
|---|---|
| **CONSOLE:** | NINTENDO SUPER FAMICOM |
| **YEAR:** | 1997 |
| **DEVELOPER:** | LENAR |
| **PUBLISHER:** | ASCII |
| **REGION:** | JAPAN |

*Gunple* was developed by Lenar, a relatively unknown company. Their most notable release was *Deadly Towers* on the NES in 1986, which received great commercial success with mixed reviews at the time.

*Gunple* is a clear-cut clone of *The Legend of Zelda: A Link to the Past*, with a few minor changes. The change that stands out the most is the way the player attacks. Instead of close-range swordplay, the player fires a pistol at enemies. With the use of the shoulder buttons, the player can strafe, locking in a certain direction while shooting. They can also punch, but doing so isn't very effective. Bullets allow for quicker attacks at longer distances with no noticeable difference in damage to a punch. The game also has a screen that's almost identical to *A Link to the Past*'s inventory screen. However, instead of items, it lists the player's available skills. Power-up items are found throughout the game, including different types of temporary guns, and a carrot — we'll explain that later.

Another contrast to *A Link to the Past* is that the game uses a lives system. If the player dies, they will be revived on the spot with their health fully recovered. If the player runs out of lives, they'll get a game over and respawn in the player's home village. The player can also find chests in dungeons. The treasures inside are converted into points once a dungeon is finished. Completing the dungeon quickly or with a lot of life remaining will award even more points. As

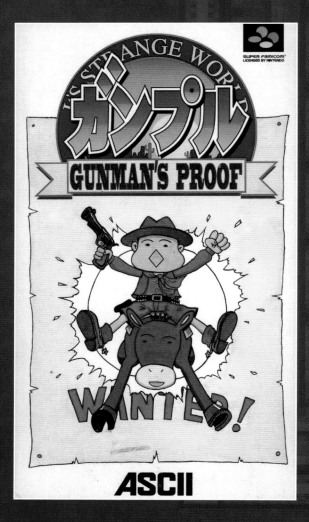

the player is using guns and doesn't have any sort of shield, attacks can be actively dodged by using the crouch button. This lets players avoid gunfire by ducking underneath bullets, though the player can't fire while crouched. The player can also gain special skills, like a charge shot used by holding down the attack button.

The game's story takes place in the year 1880. Two meteors crash into Earth on a small island near the western coast of North America. However, nobody seems to care.

It isn't until some time later, when monsters appear and attack villagers, that people start to worry. After the monsters attack their victims, they drop crests inscribed with the word 'demiseed', which comes to describe the monsters themselves. One day the game's protagonist, a young farm boy who lives in the only town on the island, finds a crash-landed miniature UFO. Two mini aliens emerge from the ship, known as Zero and Goro. They inform the player that an intergalactic criminal named Demi has escaped justice and is hiding on the island, and that they are, in fact, space sheriffs. Zero then possesses the player's body, granting him the power to fight the monsters. Together, Zero and the player must destroy Demi, thereby restoring peace to the island. During the adventure, the player meets up with Mono, another alien who crash landed while hunting Demi. Unfortunately, Mono possessed the body of a donkey named Robaton and is unable to escape it. He joins the player in his quest, and can be summoned by collecting a carrot, allowing the player to ride him and become temporarily invincible.

Graphically, it's clear that the game's backgrounds are directly influenced by *A Link to the Past*, but with character sprites closer to the minimalistic style of *Mother 3*. The comparisons between *Zelda* and *Gunple* are made even more obvious by the dungeon map screens, which are almost identical. Altogether, *Gunple* takes a lot from *A Link to the Past*, but it at least has a unique approach with its theme and gun-based gameplay.

Notable names attached to the project include Isami Nakagawa, who worked on the game's packaging artwork. Nakagawa became popular with his work on *Poguri*, a Japanese manga series. Also attached to the title was Akihito Tomisawa, a designer and

Left: *Gunple: Gunman's Proof*; right: *The Legend of Zelda: A Link to the Past*

scenario writer who previously worked at Game Freak. Several years after *Gunple*'s release, he mentioned his dissatisfaction with the final game, saying:

'Inspired by my favourite Western dramas, I wanted to make a game based on Mr Isami Nakagawa's character. However, there were several obstacles, such as communication with the company programming the game didn't go well, and it was commercialised without my consent. My ideas are reflected in a part of the basic idea, but the final release is completely different from what I had initially intended. I was deeply aware of the difficulty of making games in a freelance position. If given permission, it's a [game] I would remake.'

## Localisation

The game was likely never localised in the West because of its late publishing date. But there might be another, more sad reason, as it seems *Gunple* was in fact Lenar's last developed game. It's possible it sold too poorly for the company to remain active in the gaming market. If the company was struggling financially, publishing the title internationally would not have been an option. From the sounds of the quote from Tomisawa, it's possible they were only just able to release the game commercially in Japan, as the game appears to have been rushed out without Tomisawa's consent. Luckily, the game received a fan translation from Aeon Genesis.

SCORE: 165370 ☷ 105

LIFE: ○○○○○

 66

SCORE: 5460 ☷ 64

LIFE: ○○○○

**Found Treasure!**
**Got Bronze Mirror!**

NINTENDO FAMICOM
1989
ER:   IREM
ER:   IREM
JAPAN

omes to Japanese games,
is often a subject of contention.
games fail to be localised outside
st due to concerns that Western
s wouldn't have much interest
y hard gameplay. The NES has
n as *Castlevania* which are still
ed to be a challenge for many
One game released in Japan that
astlevania's style, but with the
of bizarre references to heavy
sic, is titled *Holy Diver*.
iver was released in 1989 by Irem,
y best known for their arcade
ch as *R-Type*, and possibly their
ntendo title *Dino City*. The game's
ffer only slightly from those of
ia, but rather than using the
Belmont whip against adversaries,
r must attack with projectile
While appearing similar, the weight
rol of the game's hero are new. His
re quicker and easier to land, and
ble to move while in mid-air.

may look just like a *Castlevania* game but believe it or not, it's
lly more unforgiving. The game is clunky even by the standards
e day. There are plenty of sections where it's as if it has
expressly (and unfairly) designed to screw you over. While
et homage to my personal favourite genre of music, heavy
playing the game is probably far more brutal than any of
usic it was inspired by.

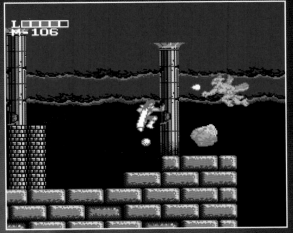
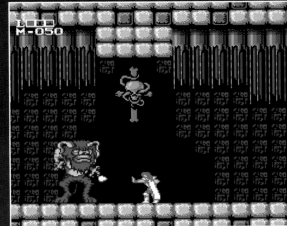

The game's narrative also makes a relatively dramatic turn from that of vampires, instead taking place in a more fantastical world of magic, with strong inspiration from rock and heavy metal. It isn't at all rare for Japanese developers to name characters after Western music, as is most recognised in franchises such as *Mega Man*.

Thanks to dire51, we have a full translation of the game's plot as seen in its instruction manual. When translated, the game's plot is as follows: 'Resurrected — The Legend of the Holy Magic King's Justice. It is the 666th year of the world of magic. The Black Slayer, Demon King of the Underground Dark Empire, has extended the world of darkness and weakened the power of King Crimson, whose wisdom has guided the world of magic for generations. The sixteenth Crimson Emperor Ronnie IV entrusted his two infant sons, Randy and Zakk, to his faithful servant Ozzy.

'The three escaped the forces from another dimension in the hope to bring light back into the world. The next seventeen years were difficult, but Randy, Zakk, and Ozzy devoted themselves to the cause of Holy Magic Justice. The Black Slayer had further extended his empire over the

countryside and the interdimensional forces were even more powerful. Randy needed to find the Royal Coat of Arms of the Crimson to battle the demons. He set out alone to carry out the will of his surrogate father Ozzy, who had [since] passed away. Thus begins the Legend of the Holy Magic King's Justice.'

Several names, such as the Black Slayer, can be seen as references to the bands Black Sabbath and Slayer. King Crimson is also named directly after the band of the same name. Emperor Ronnie is named after the late Ronnie James Dio, with the title of the game being the same as his band's debut album. Randy and Zakk are named after Randy Rhoads and Zakk Wylde, two members of Ozzy Osbourne's band, and needless to say, Ozzy is named after Osbourne himself.

The goal of *Holy Diver* is to reach the end of each stage and defeat a boss, similar to most games of its generation. The game contains a total of six stages, with each stage introducing new enemies as progress is made. Items can be obtained within each level to help improve Randy's stats and abilities, such as high jump boots or a block-breaking bracelet. Items to increase your maximum health

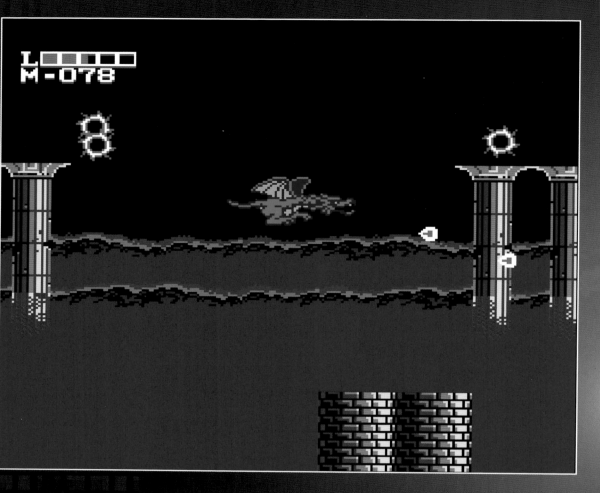

can also be found, as well as expansions to your magic meter which will be necessary for the variety of spells obtained over the first four stages.

These spells affect how the player attacks or can be used to progress further in a stage. For example, in the second level, lava will prevent the player from getting past a small jump. By using a newly obtained ice spell, it's possible to freeze the lava and stand on it to proceed. This ice can also be destroyed, helping the player to get past any walls of lava that may be streaming down.

Spells are selected from the game's pause menu and activated with the select button. When active, the spell is cast with the normal attack button. Making sure to balance the use of magic is pivotal to completing the game: although it can be employed to assist in killing enemies, some mana may need to be conserved to help progress further in the game. To help in killing enemies, for the later part of the game, Randy is able to collect an item which will transform him into a dragon. This changes the gameplay from an action platformer to something that plays more like a shoot 'em up.

An international release was hinted at briefly, but it was ultimately dropped. The game was mentioned in the US through *Electronic Gaming Monthly*'s September 1989 issue. There, *Holy Diver* was shown alongside games that would be released soon on the NES. The game's mention was small, and gave no more information on its release.

   No official reason for canning the game's localisation has ever been given, but this is a situation that difficult NES games found themselves in. It wouldn't be unusual if the game's difficulty was partly to blame for its lack of localisation, as Japanese companies often underestimated Western players. Irem's earlier NES releases mostly consist of Japan-exclusive games, so a possible lack of international networking could also have been to blame. Added to that, the game's name includes the word 'Holy', and Nintendo's stance on religious material in games on their consoles was never straightforward. Graphics appear in some stages that show religious symbols, such as crosses, as well as perhaps more controversial imagery, like foetuses. It's also possible that the game's liberal use of names from real songs, bands and musicians caused legal issues.

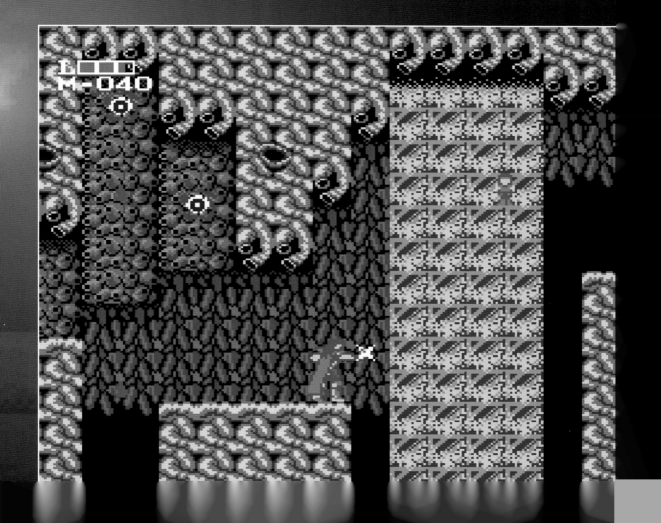

# HOLY UMBRELLA: THE RECKLESS DONDERA!!

**CONSOLE:** NINTENDO SUPER FAMICOM
**YEAR:** 1995
**DEVELOPER:** EARTHLY SOFT
**PUBLISHER:** NAXAT SOFT
**REGION:** JAPAN

Games from Japan will often reference magical weapons, generally divine in nature, used to conquer evil while bringing justice to a world in distress. These weapons range from spears sent to Earth from the heavens, to swords ordained with holy magic. A bizarre game for Super Nintendo, they opted to move away from these classic blades, and utilised something that could be more multi-purpose. That game is *Holy Umbrella: The Reckless Dondera!!*

*Holy Umbrella* was released in 1995. The game was developed by Earthly Soft, an offshoot of Tecmo, and published by Naxat Soft. *Holy Umbrella* features a combination of two different perspectives: top-down overworlds and side-on battles. Whilst in a town, the player walks around under an overhead view. While in this perspective, they can talk with residents, explore villages, purchase restorative items, and loot people's possessions.

This top-down angle changes during combat segments, and the game turns into a side-scrolling style instead. Like any action platformer, it's possible to jump or attack.

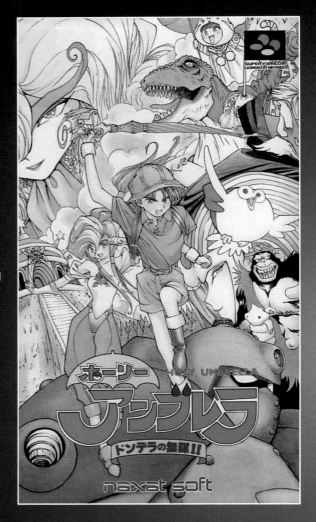

**Dazz:**
*Holy Umbrella* is absolutely hilarious. Being completely honest, the gameplay is pretty mediocre, and many other games achieve better results in trying to do the same thing. However, it's the game's story and writing which really makes it enjoyable. I was particularly impressed with the fan translation work from Aeon Genesis – would definitely recommend!

The umbrella can be used for basic attacks, but also to swing from hooks.

It's also possible to use the shoulder buttons to switch between characters, and play using an entirely different set of skills. While the protagonist wields an umbrella, the small bird Bonto is capable of fitting into smaller spaces and can double jump at the expense of their attacking capabilities. And the character Saki is able to wall jump and perform sliding kicks. Each character has their own strengths and weaknesses and switching between them during levels is pivotal.

New skills are unlocked as the player progresses, such as the ability to run and cover larger gaps with jumps, as well as being able to use the umbrella to hover. New umbrellas are also unlocked, each featuring its own special skills. This includes the ice umbrella, which can turn enemies into ice blocks, and the fire umbrella, that can create a homing projectile that can be picked up with the umbrella and thrown at any time.

The game's story is perhaps the title's biggest selling point. One day, a young Japanese boy is walking home from school when suddenly it begins to rain exceptionally hard. The boy discovers what he presumes to be an ordinary umbrella on the ground, which he assumes could shield him from the storm. But, to his surprise, upon grabbing the umbrella, the boy is sent to another world.

When he arrives in this world, the boy is attacked by Dondera Tank, an antagonist who appears throughout the boy's journey. The boy is saved by a man named Kilorn who informs him that he's in the world of Margence, specifically the country of Thurgical.

The princess of this land holds a magical power which could be used to send the boy home. However, after a seal which had been kept safe for centuries was broken by the evil Emperor Dondera, she has fallen into a weakened state. After the seal was broken, Emperor Dondera obtained magical powers, which he used to summon hordes of monsters

to attack town after town. In order to return home, the boy must seal the Dondera army, and restore the princess's power.

Kilorn then tells the boy of the Legend of the Holy Umbrella, the weapon that he now wields. Long ago, gods and goblins lived in the world. The umbrella was created from the lifeforce of a god and granted to a human in order to destroy a powerful goblin. Once the goblin was defeated, the umbrella was divided into seven holy umbrellas, and each was sealed away for protection.

To learn more, the boy must travel the world defeating the Dondera army, accompanied by Bonto, a pet bird raised by Kilorn, and Saki, a young girl looking to seek out adventure.

## Localisation

Games which feature strong Japanese themes struggle to find their way overseas. This isn't simply because publishers feel that a game's themes are too outlandish; it's also because popular culture differs across regions. Humour which is built around an

understanding of this culture doesn't always translate well, and when video games were less established, this was a major concern for publishers.

*Holy Umbrella*'s references to anime and Japanese pop culture, as well as the game's outlandish plot, didn't help make the game easy to localise. With extensive amounts of text for what is essentially a standard action platformer, the translation process would have needed more time and resources than normal and might not have been worth the effort.

Naxat Soft had no games published internationally at the time of *Holy Umbrella*'s release, with the only exception being *Serpent* on the Game Boy, and even then, they didn't publish this game by themselves. This meant that the company were probably never considering the idea in the first place, and it was purely created for the Japanese market.

You can still play *Holy Umbrella* in English, however. This is thanks once again to Aeon Genesis, who made the game a full English fan-translation patch in 2009.

# KAENA

**CONSOLE:** SONY PLAYSTATION 2
**YEAR:** 2004
**DEVELOPER:** XILAM
**PUBLISHER:** NAMCO
**REGION:** JAPAN

Video game adaptations of popular films often fail to impress when it comes to a gaming market; however, many of those games aren't actually adaptations of films that were originally intended to be games. When Chris Delaporte had his project of France's first feature-length CG movie release in 2003, it's unlikely that he believed the game adaptation would be released exclusively to the Japanese region.

Kaena: The Prophecy has strong ties to the gaming market, with work on the title beginning in 1995 after Chris left the game development studio Amazing Studio halfway through work on the company's first and only game, Heart of Darkness for the Sony PlayStation. Chris originally intended for his story to be told in the form of a game; however, plans changed and soon he was working on creating a feature-length film.

The film later received a video game adaptation which was released exclusively in Japan. We will take a brief look at the film before we talk about the game.

Kaena: The Prophecy was released to cinemas in 2003 in both French and English. It follows the story of anthropoid tree-dwellers that evolved from a tree that sprouted from the core of a ship which crash landed on a desert planet. Kaena, voiced by Kirsten Dunst in the English dub, is one of these descendants. She dreams of exploring beyond her village, something that many of the other villagers

are opposed to. Kaena decides to defy her elder's wishes and climbs to the top of the tree that spawned her race, where she meets another alien known as Opaz. Opaz, voiced by Richard Harris, is a survivor of the race that originally landed on the planet 600 years prior. With his time, he has used his technology to create a race of intelligent worms which he uses to serve his ends. He soon has Kaena attempt to retrieve the ship's core from which the tree sprouted, known as Vecanoi.

After its release, Kaena was considered both a critical and commercial failure. Many critics panned the film, stating that the plot was dull, lifeless and convoluted. Others made negative comparisons between the

イルボ 聞いて 私
大司祭を殺そうとしたと思われてるの

film and the fully CG movie *Final Fantasy: The Spirits Within* that is also seen as similarly poor. Some were critical of the character design for Kaena, with her coming across as overly sexualised.

The film's box office earnings were abysmal, with its lifetime earnings reaching just under $500,000, the vast majority of which was earned from the French theatrical release. Together, the budget for creating the movie and video game came to $26 million. Sadly, the release marks the final film work performed by renowned actor Richard Harris, who died prior to the film's much delayed release.

The film was originally intended to be created as a video game, and it's likely that during production, work on a game had already been started, as an adaptation was released a year after *Kaena*'s cinematic debut.

The game was developed by Xilam, the same studio who had worked on the film, and published in Japan by Namco in 2004.

The game makes use of the same cinematic style as its film counterpa including the use of the movie's scor While the original voice artists are of changed to accommodate the Japan language, much of the story remains the same.

Gameplay is performed from fixed camera angles in a third-person acti genre. Kaena can perform several ac as one would expect, such as simple attacks, dodging and interacting with environment. The game uses a comb system, allowing for various combo i be performed in order to defeat ener get through the stages.

By defeating monsters, the play can obtain orbs that will recharge health, points that allow them to up their weapons, or fuel for their ber meter. After the berserk meter has filled, several stronger attacks can performed.

By completing levels, it's also possible to unlock bonus content such as behind-the-scenes documentary footage of the project's creation, as well as concept art for the various creatures in the game.

Many of the game's cutscenes are taken directly from its movie counterpart, and while efforts are made to expand upon the world, with several characters giving more insight to the plot, it doesn't deviate much from the film.

Delaporte's involvement with his story's development is strong. He spent his youth as a graffiti tagger in Paris, then began his life as an artist, exploring his interests in drawing and painting. After he bought a computer, he started to work on his skills with 3D, allowing him to realise that he could use his art to tell a story.

He stated that he was drawn to video games because he felt it was the only medium that would allow him to express himself in a fantasy world. His story for *Kaena* began when he and *Kaena* co-creator Patrick Daher worked on a demo for a year without payment. This allowed him to meet Denis Friedman, who was the general director of Sony Computer France at the time. After leaving Sony, Friedman set up his own company known as Chaman. The three began to talk and learned that they each felt strongly about complementary media interaction, making a story span several different mediums.

To promote their demo, it was decided to make a two-minute 3D introduction in order to raise interest in the project. After working out an overall budget,

they ultimately reached the figure of $26 million.

To gather a crew to work on the film, the team looked for those with motivation above experience. Brought from all over Europe, many had backgrounds in video game development meaning the team had a lot of on-the-job training.

Halfway through completion of the game and film, Chaman was relieved of its duties on the story and control was given over to Xilam, a company with expertise in 3D and animation who also provided a background in video games with their releases of *The Fifth Element* video game and *Stupid Invaders*.

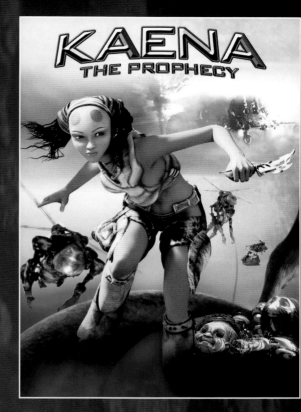

## Localisation

While we attempted to contact Chris Delaporte prior to this book's release, we received no response. As such, we have no conclusive reason as to why this game was never brought out in the US, let alone the film's origin country of France. Our assessment is one that is fairly easy to come to for those who understand the details provided.

With the film's release failing to reach an audience that would be interested in playing a game adaptation, it's likely that the game's production was considered to be of little value in the West. However, in the hopes of selling a game for its own merit, the Japanese market may have been seen as a good fit. *Kaena*'s visual style is reminiscent of that of Japanese production, and so in order for the efforts that had been made on the game to not go to waste, the team would have attempted to sell their work to a publisher in that region.

Namco showed two trailers for the film and game at the Tokyo Game Show in 2003, presumably hoping to raise some interest in the project. With the film and game being

released to little attention, the game was not a particularly strong seller there either. With the Western market being known to have reviewed the film poorly, nobody involved in the project would have been inclined to see it as a wise idea to publish the game within the region.

# KIRA KIRA STAR NIGHT DX

CONSOLE:      NINTENDO FAMICOM
YEAR:         2016
DEVELOPER:    RIKI IWASAKI
PUBLISHER:    COLUMBUS CIRCLE
REGION:       JAPAN

The homebrew community garners a lot of attention, particularly with constant demonstrations of how old hardware can still be utilised to create impressive digital media. A collaboration in Japan created titles which use the Famicom not just for gameplay, but also as a means of digital art. These games aren't officially licensed by Nintendo, as they were released well beyond the Famicom's lifecycle. The collaboration's first release in 2016, which was little more than a cartridge form of their chiptune album, was *8Bit Music Power*.

*8Bit Music Power* is, in effect, a chiptune album that uses the Famicom console to generate the music. While the cartridge features a number of minigames, these aren't the game's main draw.

The game was created in a collaboration between Columbus Circle, a hardware manufacturer in Japan, and artist Riki Iwasaki. The musical pieces featured on the cartridge were created by a number of talents in Japan, with eleven tracks in total. Artists who worked on the project include Prof. Sakamoto, Yuriko Keino and Tappy. Visualisations are included on the cartridge, with artwork that serves as a sort of screensaver whilst the album is left to play.

The game saw wide success, reaching number three in the Japanese Amazon sales charts for pre-ordered games. The team

**Dazz:**
I've always had a love of homebrew art projects – ever since I was a kid checking out the Amiga demo scene. Columbus Circle's efforts go a step further, encompassing both the visuals and music that I took an interest in while also throwing interactivity into the mix. *8Bit Music Power* may just be a menu system, but as a small indie project, it goes further than many that came before it. *Kira Kira Star Night DX* is also an incredibly basic game, but you can see the artistic talents of not just the sprite work but the whole product in every part of it: music, artwork, programming and product materials.
It's all great, though really it isn't much of a game. If you want to pick it up to play a long and enjoyable game, you'll likely be disappointed. If you have an interest in a unique art piece for the Nintendo Famicom, you'll see that in droves.

**# 04          3:07/3:46**
**♪ MASS PURPLE**
**♀ KEISHI YONAO**

PULSE ch1

PULSE ch2

TRIANGLE

NOISE

DELTAPCM

From *8-Bit Music Power*

revisited the game in 2017 in order to release a finalised version, called *8Bit Music Power Final*. This release increased the number of tracks on the cartridge from eleven to eighteen, while also refining several other elements.

While it's hard to dub these releases as 'video games', both Riki and Columbus Circle created an interactive experience on the Famicom after their first album release was a success.

*Kira Kira Star Night DX* took the team's concept further, being both musically and visually impressive, but also featuring interactive gameplay elements. The game works like most standard infinite runners, with the player controlling a young girl with a side-scrolling view. The goal is to collect stars which enter the screen in a variety of

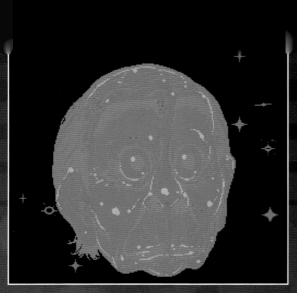

The player runs continuously and is able to jump in order to collect the stars. Patterns grow more and more complex as the game goes on, though it is only limited to two stages. To be victorious in each stage, the goal is to obtain a certain number of stars before time runs out.

The game's physics work like several classic games on the system, preventing the player from changing their jumping trajectory whilst in the air. This is the extent of gameplay for the title, making it unsurprising to hear that the game's main focus was not on the creation of complex gameplay, but instead on a demonstration of the artist's works graphically and audibly.

The reason for the lack of release in the West with these titles likely stems from their actual purpose. Being more like art pieces rather than games, the market for an artist will be with existing fans who already appreciate their creations.

Riki, the lead behind these games as well as one of the musical composers and artists, is a recognised artist in the region, having worked on an extensive number of projects ranging from mobile games, music and... adult publications (it's porn, guys).

## Localisation

Without a guaranteed market overseas, creating cartridges for what is essentially an art project would have likely been without much payoff. Versions of the cartridges would need to be created for each region that they are released in, increasing the costs of such a niche concept.

Columbus Circle, who published the titles, create hardware which is exclusively sold in Japan. Their market is entirely within the region, and it's unlikely that they felt the niche releases would be worth their time to explore expanding their distribution overseas.

TIME 065　GET/STAR 122/100　SCORE 01082

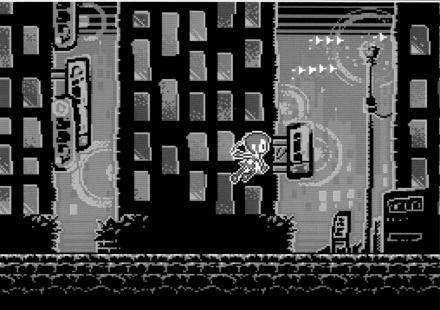

TIME 201　GET/STAR 072/090　SCORE 00493

# KLONOA BEACH VOLLEYBALL

**CONSOLE:** SONY PLAYSTATION
**YEAR:** 2002
**DEVELOPER:** NAMCO
**PUBLISHER:** NAMCO (JP), SCEE (EU)
**REGION:** JAPAN, EUROPE

*Klonoa* is a series that many hold close to their hearts. With the Japanese release of *Klonoa: Door to Phantomile* on the PlayStation in 1997 its sequel on the PlayStation 2 in 2001 as well as a variety of other games, his iconic status with Namco is a given. But *Klonoa* had another game where, like many icons in gaming's past, the developers wanted to go with a sports twist.

Released in Japan and Europe in 2002, *Klonoa Beach Volleyball* is a 2v2 volleyball sports game. As one might expect, this allows for a total of four players to compete with the use of a multitap, or with only two controllers by sharing gamepads. This is the first time a *Klonoa* game has had any multiplayer features.

The basic rules of volleyball for those who aren't aware is to simply have the ball land on the ground of your opponent's side of the net. There are more rules to it than that, but *Klonoa* goes for a relatively simplified version of this sport, opting more to be within the style of the *Klonoa* universe.

When serving, the player must strike the ball by first throwing the ball up and then jumping to hit it. Timing is extremely important in this manoeuvre, as having the ball too high to reach in a character's jump will cause the serve to fail and the opponent will receive a point.

To receive, the player must hit the X button and the direction for where on the court they would like the ball to be guided to. This can be performed twice before a strike must be made. At any time, the ball can be

intercepted with an attack instead of a pass to try and catch the opposition off guard.

Where *Klonoa Beach Volleyball* bends the rules of a typical game of volleyball to introduce *Klonoa* elements is in its special attacks. By lining three squares in a row from any direction with the nine different sections of the opponent's side of the court, unique character abilities can be used which will also grant additional points to the team. This can be made up of multiple lines at once, but the attack must land. These special attacks vary from player to player but are all stronger than a standard attack.

Each character has their own ending, but the basic premise of the game is that they are all competing in a volleyball tournament set up by Garlen, the main villain of two *Klonoa* titles on the Game Boy Advance. This is the first game in which he is playable.

This was the first game in the *Klonoa* franchise to introduce voice acting, although none of the actors used are featured in the game's credits.

## Localisation

The game only saw release in Japan and Europe, likely because of the game's sports genre. While we can't say if this was Namco's intention, sports games are often overlooked with localisations, and when it comes to distribution, creating a PAL version of the title allows the game to be sold across a wider audience. It's possible that Namco felt that the game was not marketable to a US audience.

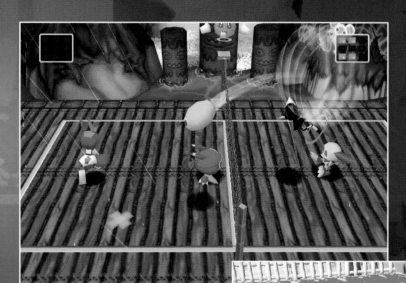

| CONSOLE: | NINTENDO SUPER FAMICOM, NINTENDO WII U |
|---|---|
| YEAR: | 1994 |
| DEVELOPER: | SQUARESOFT |
| PUBLISHER: | SQUARESOFT |
| REGION: | JAPAN |

When many think of Squaresoft, they will immediately jump to the *Final Fantasy* series, a collection of RPGs with a loose common theme running through them. The company has historically been the master of RPGs, particularly when it comes to the SNES's library of games, having published several of the bestselling and highest rated titles on the platform for the genre. However, Squaresoft created several standalone games which never had a Western release, including one combining multiple stories.

That game is *Live A Live*.

*Live A Live* was published in 1994 for the SNES and features seven different playable characters with their own aesthetic and stories. Typical of the RPG genre, the game focuses on having the player explore various locations through overworld navigation, talking with a variety of different NPCs, exploring dungeons and gaining experience in order to level up. Unlike most RPGs, however, the majority of the game's battles are plot driven and fixed, with only one having any form of random encounters.

These battles play out similarly to turn-based tactical titles: from a top-down perspective on a seven-by-seven grid. While the player is able to perform basic attacks, several characters also have their own unique skills. Rather than using magic with a dedicated MP meter, as is standard for many RPGs, instead some skills can take multiple turns to charge. During this period, the player cannot move and can be interrupted by enemies, cancelling the attack.

Some attacks can alter tiles, causing a variety of effects when a character is standing on them, such as taking fire damage on a burning tile or receiving a status effect.

**Matt Barnes:**
It's always a joy to find a game that exceeds expectations. There aren't many games in *Region Locked* that we play where you wonder how they did it. I had no idea about *Live A Live* until the other guys suggested playing it. I expected a fantastic game along the lines of any RPG but with the limitations of a SNES game. Even being told that it was by Squaresoft and it has seven playable characters, I wasn't expecting each style to be as radically different as they were, even down to the gameplay in each one. Basically, seven games on one cartridge! Definitely worth playing through!

When a character's life reaches zero they are knocked out, rather than being immediately killed. It's possible to revive the downed character by simply healing them; however, if the downed character is attacked, they will be removed from the fight altogether. After the fight is concluded, they are returned to the player with full life.

The game's basic premise follows heroes throughout time. During each period of history, there has been a hero who has fought for justice. Each of the game's seven different protagonists has their own dedicated chapter, which can be chosen in any desired order, with each one working as a sort of standalone game. Chapters take place across a wide span of time, ranging from prehistoric times to modern day and even the distant future.

Though the gameplay remains largely the same, each chapter does feature some variation.

## Caveman Chapter — Contact — Pogo

During the prehistoric era, a young woman named Bel has escaped from a tribe seeking to sacrifice her to their deity, O-D-O, a living tyrannosaurus-rex. She escapes to the south, hiding

amongst another tribe's dwellings. When she is discovered by Pogo and his friend Gori, he helps her to hide from his tribe. After being discovered, the three are exiled, and must fend for themselves alone.

In a time before speech, this portion of the game involves no dialogue, instead having characters communicate through visual expressions.

## Kung-Fu Master Chapter — Inheritance — Xin Shan Quan

Set in ancient China, in his old age, a powerful kung fu master has decided he needs to pass on his wisdom. He proceeds to gather three potential young protégés. The player trains the students through three stages. One for endurance, one for agility and one for strength. Granted four training sessions per stage, the player must decide how to split them amongst the three trainees.

## Ninja Chapter — Secret Orders — Oboro

Set in feudal Japan, a young ninja of the Enma clan, Oboro, is sent to infiltrate the castle of Ode Iou. Ode has assembled a team of powerful evildoers and plans to plunge Japan into chaos. Oboro must first free one of Ode's prisoners, said to be the only one capable of stabilising Japan, before facing off against the villains. The player has the option of sneaking through the castle, avoiding the majority of the fights or they can simply cut down any opponents that stand in their way. The player can activate a cloak of invisibility to avoid detection from the patrolling guards; however, they are unable to move when in cover. There are numerous possible paths to choose from, some more dangerous than others.

## Cowboy Chapter — Wandering — Sundown Kid

In the American Old West, a lone, quiet cowboy with lightning-fast gun skills travels the land: the Sundown Kid. After his home was raided by a gang of outlaws, the guilt of not being able to protect the town drove him to place a bounty on his own head so that he might find a place to die. Stopping off in Success Town, he takes on the burden of protecting it and its villagers from a bandit gang named the Crazy Bunch.

The player has to collect resources that can be used as traps for when the bandits arrive, with the player selecting which NPC sets up which traps. Several character names in this section possibly make reference to popular western films, with the Sundown Kid being a reference to *Butch Cassidy and the Sundance Kid*, while young child Billy is a reference to Billy the Kid.

## Wrestler Chapter — The Strongest — Masaru

Taking place in modern-day Japan, Masaru dreams of becoming the strongest person on earth. He enters a global fighting tournament so that he can learn more about combat styles from around the world, defeating each opponent to learn their skills and earning the title of the strongest person in the world.

Unlike the other chapters of the game, this chapter has no overworld exploration. Instead, Masaru must compete in a series of fights, including against a character clearly referencing Hulk Hogan, and with dialogue screens like those seen in *Street Fighter II*.

## Mecha Chapter — Flow — Akira Tadokoro

Taking place in Japan in the near future, kidnappings are occurring thanks to a biker gang called the Crusaders. Their intentions are unknown, but an orphan with psychic powers, Akira Tadokoro, sets out to rescue a child from his orphanage who has been taken by the gang. Akira soon learns of a government conspiracy involving mechs.

It's highly likely that this chapter has been inspired by the manga and influential anime film *Akira*, a story involving psychic powers and biker gangs in the near future.

## Science Fiction Chapter — Mechanical Heart — Cube

In the distant future, a robot on a transport ship headed to Earth with a Behemoth in the cargo hold gets wrapped up in a crisis situation.

The ship featured in this chapter is called *Cogito Ergosum*, a Latin phrase meaning 'I think, therefore I am', Descartes' famous philosophical statement that represents

self-identity and awareness. The ship's pilot, Kirk, is named after James T. Kirk from *Star Trek*, and Corporal Darth is likewise named after Darth Vader from *Star Wars*.

This chapter features almost no combat besides the final boss. An optional minigame can be played, however, in which the player must defeat nine waves of enemies while taking on the role of 'Captain Square'.

Some chapters have multiple endings and the player is able to replay them in order to achieve the results they desire. These endings can be decided by something as simple as dying, and each ending has an impact on the game's finale.

**SPOILER ALERT!** After completing all seven of the original chapters, it should become apparent that the boss of each chapter is a variation of the same demon: Odio. An eighth story is unlocked at this point.

## Medieval Chapter — King of Demons — Oersted

Oersted, a hero in the land of Lucretia, and his friend Straybow compete in a tournament to win Princess Alicia's hand in marriage. The night after Oersted's victory, Alicia is kidnapped by the Demon King. Oersted and his friend embark on a mission to rescue her.

Meeting the heroes of old who previously defeated the Demon King, Hash and Uranus, Oersted and Straybow are convinced to fight him once again. The team battles and defeats the Demon King, but not without the loss of Hash, who passes away from the plague. Unable to find Alicia, and after Straybow is seemingly crushed by falling rocks, Oersted and Uranus return home defeated.

The night of their return, Oersted is tricked into killing the King of Lucretia by the Demon King, causing others to accuse

him of being the Demon King himself. After escaping imprisonment, Oersted returns to the mountain to find Straybow alive and well. Out of jealousy, Straybow sold his soul so that he may become the next Demon King, and thus he was the one who tricked Oersted into the act of murder. After defeating Straybow, and rescuing Princess Alicia, she professes her love for Straybow, blaming Oersted for Straybow's descent into madness. She then commits suicide. Unable to handle the events surrounding him, Oersted makes the decision to become the next Demon King himself, donning the name Odio. Seeking out revenge, he kills everybody in the land.

## The Final Chapter

For the game's final chapter, the player can decide which character to take control of. After the events of the previous chapter, Oersted summons the heroes of the game for a final showdown. The player must recruit the six other characters and defeat Oersted in his final demon form. After being defeated, Oersted returns to his original form, and requests the player kill him. After refusing, Oersted attacks again, forcing each protagonist to defeat the incarnation of Odio from their respective chapter. After taking each one down, the heroes all explain their reasons for fighting; moved by their words, Oersted returns them back to their time periods, warning them that anybody is capable of becoming a demon if they are filled with enough hatred. He passes away, and Lucretia is returned to normal.

With the final chapter of the game, if the player chooses Oersted as the lead role, he will take on the form of each boss in their time period, defeating the heroes in each one. Oersted is then left to a world empty of human life while the credits roll.

A recurring dark comedic joke in the form of a father and son duo with the surname Watanabe also appears in each chapter. In most cases, the father will die, leaving the son distraught and worse off, providing nothing to the plot and only lending itself to very dark humour.

*Live A Live* was directed by Takashi Tokita after he had just completed work as a lead designer on *Final Fantasy IV*. After the game's release, he would then go on to direct *Chrono Trigger*, *Parasite Eve* and *Chocobo Racing*.

Tokita stated that by splitting the game into different chapters, it was easier to create seven shorter stories at once with different teams rather than a single story playing throughout a long game. Each chapter in the game has its own unique style, designed by different popular manga artists, including Ryōji Minagawa, Gosho Aoyama and Kazuhiko Shimamoto.

The game's soundtrack was solely composed by Yoko Shimomura, renowned for her work on *Kingdom Hearts*, *Final Fantasy XV*, and various Mario RPGs.

References to *Live A Live* can be found in the *Final Fantasy Legends* mobile titles, or *Final Fantasy Dimensions* in the West; the game's final boss, Odio, makes an appearance as a summon in the game *Final Fantasy Dimensions II*, while Oersted appears as a boss in *Final Fantasy Legends: Crystal of Space-Time*. The Nintendo DS game *Theatrhythm Final Fantasy: Curtain Call* also has two downloadable songs from the game: 'Birds in the Sky, Fish in the River' and 'Megalomania'. During Megalomania's stage, Oersted and Straybow can be seen fighting on the Demon King's Mountain. These would be the only time that a Western market would be exposed to any content from *Live A Live*.

*Live A Live* received a Virtual Console release in Japan through Nintendo's Wii U in 2015, and the New Nintendo 3DS in 2016.

## Localisation

Because the seven artists that were used to create the game were working for Shogakukan publishing at the time of the game's original release, Shogakukan

holds partial rights over the game. This made an official rerelease a challenge for Square, but it also helps to determine a factor for why the game never saw localisation.

No official reason was provided by Square as a company, but various tweets from Takashi Tokita regarding the game's VC release explain how the game's rights are still handled, as well as how instrumental community interest was in the game's revival.

However, it is *also* possible that the game didn't manage to gain favour due to being released mere months after Square's smash-hit game *Final Fantasy VI*, resulting in Square as a company having little interest in working through the legal process.

In 2011, Spencer of Siliconera asked Takashi Tokita if he would ever consider a remake of the title. Tokita responded, 'Definitely, if the fans request it, I'd love to do that. In my experience, *Live A Live*'s

omnibus style of multiple chapters was a learning experience and an element I brought over to [*Final Fantasy IV:*] *The After Years*. That's why that game has multiple chapters, as well.'

The game received a fan translation in 2001 from Gideon Zhi of translation group Aeon Genesis as a project that he had undertaken for a business class. The resulting patch was widely considered to be usable, allowing the game to be played, though in an unpolished state. In 2008, a new translation was made after Gideon took on help regarding the technical portion of the patch so that he could instead concentrate on writing.

Considered to be the definitive work of the translation group, the 2.0 Deluxe release of the translation doesn't just fix a large number of bugs present in the original fan translation, but also introduces a unique font for each chapter as well some other cosmetic flair.

| | |
|---|---|
| **CONSOLE:** | SONY PLAYSTATION |
| **YEAR:** | 1998 |
| **DEVELOPER:** | ASMIK ACE ENTERTAINMENT |
| **PUBLISHER:** | ASMIK ACE ENTERTAINMENT |
| **REGION:** | JAPAN |

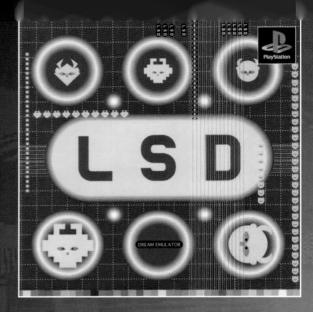

In October of 1998, Asmik Ace Entertainment developed and published a game that to this day still perplexes the gaming community. *LSD: Dream Emulator* is an obscure title that nobody in the West could play at the time of its release but has since picked up a small cult following.

The game's purpose is simple: to explore. With no interactive objects, *LSD* simply allows the player to move around the dreamlike environments with basic navigation controls. However, it is possible to teleport to different environments by walking into various objects, which includes pretty much everything, even walls. This teleportation is known as 'linking', and it's believed that walking into living creatures or bizarre items will link the player to more obscure locations.

This surreal world was conceived by the mind of Hiroko Nishikawa, an artist at Asmik Ace Entertainment, who kept a journal of her dreams for over a decade. Osamu Sato,

the game's director, took those dreams and conceived mechanics that would let people explore such a world.

In this game, dreams come to an end automatically after around ten minutes. There are other ways of ending a dream, however, such as falling off a cliff edge. After a dream has ended and the player has 'woken up', they are presented with a graph. This graph is designed to keep track of the player's dreams and will reveal the overall theme of the dreams they've had. These

**Greg:**
Closer to art than an actual game, *LSD: Dream Emulator* is a very… interesting look into the minds of Sato and Nishikawa. The variety of areas and textures in the game appeals directly to the part of the brain that craves discovery. Despite its aged graphics, the nightmares can be genuinely unnerving, with mysterious faceless characters quite literally losing their heads, and families hanging from lampposts. We played this game together passing the controller between dreams and I would highly recommend it; by the end it almost felt like the game knew who was playing…

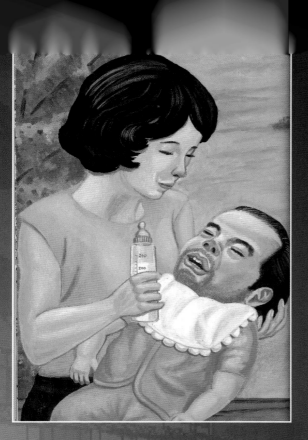

are tracked as 'upper', 'downer', 'static' and 'dynamic'. It is also believed that previously played dreams can have an impact on the player's subsequent dreams. The graph may be based on the actions taken while sleeping. But which slot on the graph is filled seems almost arbitrary, as constantly moving or staying still has little effect on the dynamic and static trackers.

Environments found in the game can change on a regular basis. The dream world is made up of a base map that doesn't change, though the elements within it move freely, and tunnels allow the player to travel between areas. Navigation is inconsistent, however, as walking into the same object multiple times can teleport the player to different locations. On top of that, the textures in each environment can also change. These textures may even change while the player is near them, such as eyes appearing on walls that stare at the player.

After a number of days dreaming, the game allows the player to re-explore old dreams. This is one of the only ways to see the same dream twice, as the game's randomised nature doesn't allow for easily repeated interactions. While normal dreams last ten minutes, revisited dreams only last around three minutes.

Some dreams are non-interactive videos that the player can watch. These are so far-fetched that they only increase the confusing nature of the game. Some dreams even remove the video aspect altogether and are simply black screens with Japanese characters covering them. These screens tell stories and often make little sense.

The game's producer, Osamu Sato, wrote the soundtrack for the game himself. The game contains over 500 different patterns of music, which change depending on the dream's theme. These patterns are just a number of variations of the same simple

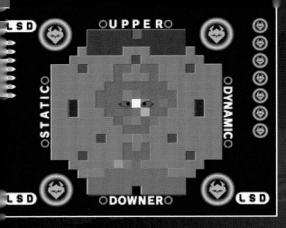

unes, and use a collection of different electronic sound effects. The soundtrack was given away with the limited-edition release of the game as a bonus CD called *Lucy in the Sky with Dynamites*. This is a parody of the Beatles track 'Lucy in the Sky with Diamonds', which was also known for having the acronym 'LSD', albeit unintentionally (despite the rumours that the song was inspired by the drug).

A book containing excerpts of the dream journal written by Nishikawa was also given away with this limited-edition release. Each excerpt is presented alongside a piece of artwork created by various artists.

A second album of the game's soundtrack was released on two CDs in Japan under the Japanese techno label Music Mine Inc. Titled *LSD and Remixes*, this soundtrack features not only music found in the game, but also remixes performed by multiple artists. This includes British IDM pioneer Mike Paradinas, Finnish jazz performer Jimi Tenor, and Japanese DJ Ken Ishii.

Due to the game's trippy nature, many people incorrectly took its title, *LSD*, to be a reference to the drug lysergic acid diethylamide, also known by the street name acid, or LSD. The title is given different meanings throughout the game and related material, using acronyms such as 'In Life the

Sensuous Dream' and 'In Limbo, the Silent Dream' but it is never stated to be a direct reference to drugs.

It is commonly believed that *LSD* has no ending. Some players found a file titled 'ENDING.STR' on the game's disk, which is a type of PlayStation video file. This led to discovering that, after going through 365 different dreams, the game will play this file. However, the video itself is confusing and seems to have no relevance to anything in the game. It's speculated that the video symbolises a Hatsuyume. In Japanese culture, a Hatsuyume is the first dream somebody has in a new year. It's considered good luck to dream of three things in particular: Mount Fuji, a hawk and an aubergine — the three items shown in the game's ending. After the clip has finished, the day counter seen on the game's main menu will reset back to day one.

The game received a cult following after Let's Play videos began to surface on YouTube in 2009. Players were intrigued by the strange and confusing worlds they were shown. One fan of the game, Figglewatts, even created an unofficial remake of the game called *LSD Revamped*. Still in early alpha, the unofficial remake plans to introduce new features such as original areas and mod support.

## Localisation

The reason for the game's lack of localisation in the West has never been confirmed. However, it's possible that there simply wasn't a market for this type of game in the 1990s. Osamu Sato, the game's director, had previously created a game called *Eastern Mind: The Lost Souls of Tong-Nou*. The game had a similarly bizarre presentation and is believed to have sold poorly in the West. The title even had a sequel, *Chu-Teng*, that never left Japan. It's possible that the poor sales of *Eastern Mind* in the West indicated that it wouldn't be worth the investment to release *LSD* or *Chu-Teng* outside of Japan. However, *LSD* did receive a digital release on PSN in 2010, again restricted only to Japan. With digital distribution allowing for publishers to release region-locked titles to wider audiences for little investment, it seems curious that the game never made it to digital stores in the West.

The once Japan-exclusive *Cho Aniki: Kyuukyoku Muteki Ginga Saikyou Otoko* was released on the US PlayStation Store in 2010. Interestingly, the game was untouched, and had all of its original Japanese text intact. This seems to relate to Sony's policies regarding PlayStation 1 Classics on the PlayStation Store. Previously, Capcom had issues with a Sony policy that didn't allow changes to be made to PlayStation 1 Classics. Capcom wanted to modify several textures to remove previous product placements in *Mega Man Legends*, but ended up resolving the legal issues with the copyright holders instead. *Cho Aniki*'s lack of translation lines up with this policy and could mean that Japanese games aren't allowed to update their contents if they're published as PlayStation 1 Classics in the US. If that's the case, *LSD* has several text-heavy dreams that would need to remain Japanese assuming it was brought to the American PlayStation Store. If Osamu Sato believed that understanding these messages was an integral part of *LSD*'s experience, he may have opted not to bring the game to the West.

We contacted Sato to comment on the game's lack of localisation, hoping that he could give us some insight. Sato confirmed to us that *LSD* never came to the West because it was expected to sell poorly outside of Japan. However, he didn't know why the game was never brought to the American PlayStation Store, and implied that decision was down to Sony.

# MARIO & WARIO

**CONSOLE:** NINTENDO SUPER FAMICOM
**YEAR:** 1993
**DEVELOPER:** GAME FREAK
**PUBLISHER:** NINTENDO
**REGION:** JAPAN

Anyone who's familiar with Nintendo's Mario knows that the plumber has a plethora of games under his belt. Since the franchise is well known and easy to sell, Nintendo uses Mario to experiment with different genres, and any new ideas they might be cooking up. That's why, when the Super Nintendo was given a mouse peripheral in 1991, Mario was chosen to demonstrate the peripheral's capabilities in *Mario Paint*. Although many Westerners got to play *Mario Paint*, Nintendo created another mouse-based Mario game that never made it to the West: *Mario & Wario*. Before we go into why the game was never localised, let's take a look at the game itself.

   *Mario & Wario* follows the story of Mario and his friends exploring a magical forest. Their goal is to find a fairy which is said to bring happiness to those who meet it. While in the woods trying to confirm the legend, Luigi gets lost from the group, and so they all split up to try and find him. During the search, Wario drops a bucket from the sky which becomes stuck on Mario's head. Wanda, the magical fairy that Mario and his friends are searching for, decides to intervene and help them out. Unable to remove the bucket due to being too weak, Wanda takes it upon herself to help guide Mario and his friends through a series of puzzles to help reunite them with the lost Luigi.

   The gameplay revolves around using the mouse to control Wanda. Clicking on objects has Wanda interact with them,

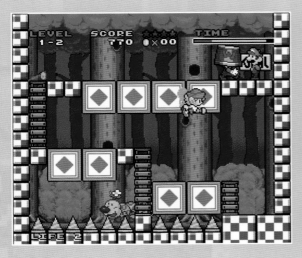

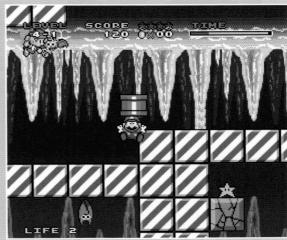

allowing the player to create a safe passage for the characters. The main aim is to have them meet up with Luigi at the end of each stage, as he has the strength to remove the bucket. Because of several key elements, the gameplay is often compared to the *Mario vs. Donkey Kong* series. Characters walk forwards of their own volition, so making sure they don't walk into danger is important. Each character has their own set speed, with Mario being faster than Peach, and Yoshi being faster than Mario.

The game also includes a bonus game at the end of each stage where the player must use Wanda to hit Wario with a hammer. Each time Wario is hit, the player earns a coin.

There isn't a whole lot to this game that would make it particularly complicated to play, but levels do get progressively more difficult as time goes on. The game gradually introduces new blocks, includes additional enemies, and makes levels more complex, requiring the player to multitask efficiently.

*Mario & Wario* was designed by Pokémon creator Satoshi Tajiri, and was developed by the team at Game Freak. This makes *Mario & Wario* the second title Game Freak ever created with Nintendo after *Yoshi* on the NES. Their next time developing

with Nintendo would be for the renowned Pokémon games. In fact, *Mario & Wario* even shares the same composer as Pokémon, Junichi Masuda. Many people also believe that the music played in World 7 of *Mario & Wario* sounds similar to the Route 24 & 25 track heard in the first generation of Pokémon games.

*Mario & Wario*'s imprint on the history of the Mario series is very small — and it's rarely mentioned in the West, if at all. The only references we could find in Western releases were in *Super Smash Bros. Melee*,

*Kirby Super Star*, and *Pokémon*. In *Melee*, the description for the Bucket Trophy makes mention of the game and its goal; in *Kirby*, the bucket that falls on Mario's head is a collectable treasure; and in *Pokémon Red and Blue*, when examined, the Super Nintendo in the Copycat's house in Saffron City states the game on screen shows Mario with a bucket on his head. This reference was even carried forward to games' remakes: *Fire Red* and *Leaf Green*.

## Localisation

Bringing *Mario & Wario* to the West would have been a quick and easy process, as the game's text is written entirely in English. So why was it never localised? The answer to why *Mario & Wario* never made it to the West may lie in the game's sales figures. The title sold relatively poorly in Japan. This was likely related to the underwhelming sales of *Mario Paint*, which also used the Super Nintendo mouse peripheral. *Mario & Wario* sold roughly 500,000 copies in Japan, over 200,000 less than *Mario Paint* in the

region. To give some perspective, *Super Mario World*, which came out three years prior, sold 3.5 million units in Japan alone. Since the game required the SNES mouse to function, the game would also need to be sold at a higher price if it were bundled with the peripheral. In Japan, *Mario & Wario* was sold bundled with the mouse for 9500 yen, which in 1993 was about 100 US dollars. Since most SNES games were $50 at the time, this would have been a hard sell in the US market.

Evidence shows that the game almost did receive a release outside of Japan, however. A preview for the game can be found in the September 1993 edition of *Nintendo Power*, which compared the game to *Lemmings*. Kellogg's cereals also ran a competition that showed the box art of *Mario & Wario* among its prizes. Within the entry form though, no publishing date had been set, and the game simply had an estimated release of '1994'.

Thanks to SNES Central for the information on the Kellogg's competition that ran for the game.

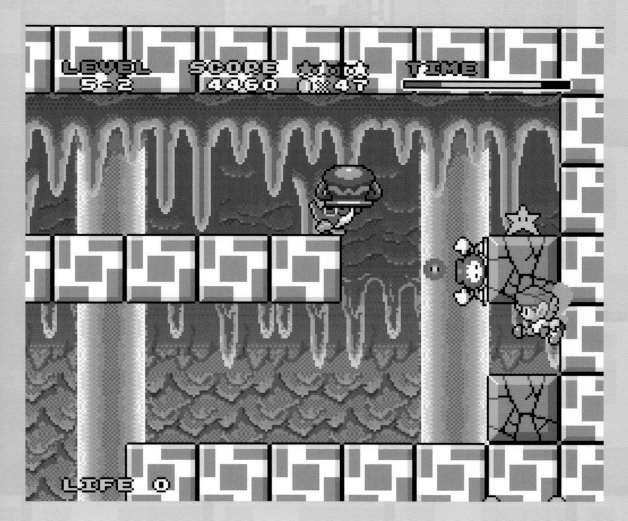

| CONSOLE: | NINTENDO SUPER FAMICOM |
|---|---|
| YEAR: | 1996 |
| DEVELOPER: | NINTENDO RESEARCH & DEVELOPMENT 2 |
| PUBLISHER: | NINTENDO |
| REGION: | JAPAN |

Before his work on the *Zelda* series, Eiji Aonuma worked as a graphic designer at Nintendo. He managed to get an interview at the company after graduating, and was able to show examples of his work directly to *Zelda* creator Shigeru Miyamoto. Aonuma managed to impress and was put to work making pixel art for Nintendo games. Before he got the chance to work on a *Zelda* game, Aonuma had the opportunity to direct his own Nintendo title: *Marvelous: Another Treasure Island*.

*Marvelous* was released towards the end of 1996, and while it's easy to draw clear similarities between *Marvelous* and the *Zelda* series, their differences become clear almost immediately. Rather than focusing on action, the game has more of an emphasis on puzzles. Combining popular gameplay mechanics of its time, the game feels like a combination of *Zelda* and *The Lost Vikings*, with PC adventure game elements mixed in. Taking control of three characters in a team named by the player, the aim is to solve various puzzles and traverse further across the world. To do this, it's required to use all three characters as both a team and individually, utilising their unique traits and items.

At any time while walking around, the player can investigate items both near and far with the use of a cursor. This often changes the view to a more detailed first-person perspective where more information can be given to the player. This can range from talking to characters or investigating objects. During these screens it's also possible to use items or make use of combined team actions to proceed. This could be positioning characters to lift or push objects that lie in their way, or

performing unique actions to suit their situation, such as stacking to reach things. Items can also change gameplay. For example, one character will obtain a baseball glove and ball which can hit various items and enemies, something which up to this point in the game is not possible.

The game's plot follows three young boys: Dion, Jack and Max. Dion is a heart-of-gold rascal who tends to lead, Jack is considered the intellectual, and Max is the strongest. The trio are camping with their class on a mysterious island when they uncover a disturbance. A legendary pirate, Captain Maverick, has hidden treasure on the island known as 'Marvelous', which can only be found by those willing to complete supposedly unsolvable puzzles. The boys use their wits to prove the legend wrong, while also discovering a band of pirates who want the treasure for themselves. While sounding simple, a variety of bizarre and imaginative situations unfold throughout the game.

Before the game's full retail release, another game in the series was published through Nintendo's Satellaview system. *BS Marvelous: Time Athletic* came out at the start of 1996, followed by the game's full retail release. The retail game was followed by yet another Satellaview game called *BS Marvelous: Camp Arnold*. These Satellaview releases act more as side quests to the main game. Rather than follow the standard style of adventure gameplay, the titles are more akin to a children's activity known as 'Stamp Rallies' in Japan. The goal is to visit a list of locations on a sheet of paper and use various stamps located at each one to mark them off.

The Satellaview games also made use of a system known as SoundLink, which streams the soundtrack to the console rather than storing it locally. While this has led to issues in the past with Satellaview titles losing their soundtracks, old recordings

of the *BS Marvelous* games can be found online by YouTube user 1983parrothead. The *Marvelous* games also made use of the SoundLink system to provide voice acting in these side games.

During an interview with Spike regarding *The Legend of Zelda: A Link Between Worlds*, Aonuma mentioned how *Marvelous* came to be. Aonuma was inspired by *A Link to the Past*, and credits the title with sparking his interest in game development. He felt that changing the game world by cutting grass and bushes, even for a short period, was something special. This experience led to his work on *Marvelous*. *Marvelous*'s resemblance to *Zelda* was so apparent that after seeing the project, Miyamoto proclaimed, 'If you really want to make a *Zelda* game that bad, why don't you just actually make a *Zelda* game.' The next title Aonuma would help design was *The Legend of Zelda: Ocarina of Time*.

## Localisation

When Aonuma was asked if he would ever revisit *Marvelous* or consider publishing the title outside of Japan, he stated, 'It would be cool to have it on the Virtual Console, but we'd also have to localise the game, so it might be kind of difficult. And we'd have to do it with superimposed subtitles, because we can't actually remake the game at this point, and actually get the data.' Despite this, a fan translation of the game was created by DackR and Tashi. This patch has been updated several times, and its latest release has totally converted all Japanese into English. This includes graphical changes, as well as the dialogue. Aonuma's statement of not being able to edit the title is of course proven false by the mere existence of this patch, but his reluctance is still understandable. Virtual Console releases which were originally exclusive to Japan tend to keep their original Japanese script. This has few exceptions, though games like *Monster World IV* did receive a full translation.

The reason for the game's lack of release outside of Japan is likely due to the Nintendo 64's release. *Marvelous: Another Treasure Island* was published in 1996 after the Nintendo 64 had already been released, and as a result, a full translation and release on the dying Super Nintendo would have been an unwise move. With that said, the game was featured in *Nintendo Power* and received a full four pages of coverage. In this article, Dion was given a different name, and was instead called Dino. This could indicate that plans were made for the game to be taken overseas.

Another interesting aspect to this story is that Nintendo may have also had plans to continue the series. *Navi Trackers*,

Dude, we're pirates!
We're not letting you
out!

A zipper..?

a sidegame available in the Japanese release of *Zelda: Four Swords Adventures*, plays similarly to the original Satellaview *Marvelous* releases. It sees the players competing to collect stamps before their opponents. This sidegame even has voice acting. Dark Linkaël from The Cutting Room Floor discovered unused data within this segment of the game which reveals some very interesting information. The data includes character icons of Dion in various colours, an unused render of Ms. Gina with some Luck Rocks which would have appeared on the television to show the players where each stamp would be, and exact replicas of maps found within *BS Marvelous: Time Athletic*.

Alright, let's combine
our power!

# THE MYSTERIOUS MURASAME CASTLE

**CONSOLE:** NINTENDO FAMICOM DISK SYSTEM
**YEAR:** 1986
**DEVELOPER:** NINTENDO
**PUBLISHER:** NINTENDO
**REGION:** JAPAN

Back in 1986, Nintendo created a hardware expansion for the Famicom known as the Famicom Disk System, or FDS for short. This attachment allowed developers to create games using a higher capacity floppy diskette. The FDS never saw a release outside of Japan, and as a result, a number of its titles were not taken overseas.

One of these titles was *The Mysterious Murasame Castle*. The game was prominent enough for Nintendo to make a minigame based on it for the Wii U launch title, *Nintendo Land*. It was eventually released to the international market on the 3DS Virtual Console in 2014. But this was twenty-eight years after the game's initial release, and to little fanfare. So why did it take so long for *Murasame Castle* to reach the West, and why is it still so obscure? First, let's take a look at the game.

The game's plot takes place during the Edo period of Japan. During a stormy night, an alien falls from the sky and infiltrates a castle known as Murasame Castle. Within the castle is a stone statue called Murasame which the alien brings to life. From there, the alien's power extends to the four other neighbouring castles and takes over their lords. Each lord gains a sphere that summons ninjas and monsters, which are used to attack villagers. The player assumes the role of Takamaru, an apprentice samurai, who is sent to investigate the strange

**Greg:**
If you're a glutton for punishment then this game is for you. It's fast, it's unfair, it's fun but it can get fucking fucked. Fuck! If *Contra* is like your house burning down, *Murasame Castle* is Mount Vesuvius blotting out the sun and permanently reshaping the Earth. The level of difficulty is unreasonably high. Other than you, the floor and the walls (and I'm not even sure you can trust them), everything else is trying as hard as possible to make you stop playing. That said, if somehow you make it to the end, it is guaranteed to be one of the most satisfying gaming experiences of your life.

occurrences. Takamaru must defeat the lords of each castle before taking on the alien that powers them.

Work started on the game when the team behind Zelda experimented with their engine. Their experiments led them to increase the action elements by adding more speed to the engine. *Murasame* was the end result of these experiments.

The gameplay is similar to that of the original *Legend of Zelda*, featuring a top-down angle with no screen scrolling. In contrast to *Zelda*, however, *Murasame Castle* follows a linear path and has time limits for each level. Areas are made up of two sections: the approach from outside of a castle, followed by the infiltration of said castle. The RPG elements from *Zelda* are also removed. While the game features levels that lead onto one another, the levels themselves have branching paths that can lead to dead ends and loops through the stage.

Takamaru has two weapons at his disposal: his katana and an infinite supply of throwing knives. The katana, used for close-range attacks, can also deflect various projectiles. The shurikens can be upgraded through various collectables found throughout the game, but these are lost whenever the player loses a life. Collectables can include fireballs,

and a bladed wheel. Takamaru has additional skills that can be used, such as an invisibility cloak that makes him invulnerable for a short period, and a lightning bolt that kills all enemies on screen.

The player is also able to obtain additional lives by rescuing damsels found within the game's castles. Sometimes, however, these can be demons in disguise ready to ambush the player. The demon will follow them throughout the castle from screen to screen and will only stop if killed. The game is considered to be incredibly difficult due to the high volume of enemies that appear on the screen at one time, their speed of attack, and the fact that demons can appear when a player is attempting to gain extra lives. The enemies are primarily made up of figures from Japanese culture, such as feudal ninjas, samurai, hannya and tenguu.

While the game lets players attack enemies using the katana at close range, once they reach the second level this becomes a relatively meaningless approach, as several enemies will explode when they're hit. Additionally, enemies will start to throw fireballs at the player which the katana is unable to deflect.

The spike in difficulty between levels is extreme, as it only takes three hits before a

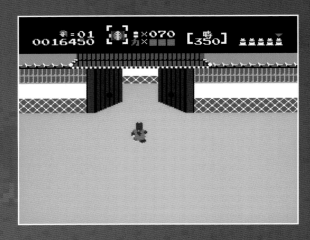

life is lost. Several enemies that can only be hit with the precise timing of a ranged attack begin to appear within the castles. This also has to be done while dodging a large number of projectiles being thrown at the player. Enemies will often change patterns on each play through, making memorisation a tricky task.

## Localisation

The reason for the game's initial lack of localisation has never been officially stated. Many believe the game's intrinsic Japanese theming made Nintendo question if it would appeal to Western players. It's possible that Nintendo simply considered the game too difficult for non-Japanese players. The title was also delayed during development, originally intended to be released alongside the Famicom Disk System and Zelda. *Murasame Castle* sold roughly 610,000 units in Japan, but only had about 150,000 downloads via Disk Writer Kiosks. These kiosks enabled users to overwrite their Famicom discs with new games for a cheaper price. Nintendo might have used kiosks to gauge player interest, as *Murasame Castle* had some of the lowest rewrite figures on the system. For comparison, the Japanese *Super Mario Bros. 2*, known as *The Lost Levels* in the West, had over 1 million rewrites from kiosks.

To get a better idea of what might have happened, we asked an ex-localiser for their opinion on the game. They told us that a lack of localisation was probably due to the game's Japanese theme. In the late 1980s, the US market didn't buy overtly Japanese titles enough to justify localising them. However, the market shifted over the years, allowing for online distribution, and digital publishing costs are much lower than they are for physical media. And with eShop accessibility, there's a greater chance of niche titles being released digitally at reduced cost and risk for the publisher. Another example of this can be seen with *Fatal Frame: Maiden of Black Water*, which was originally a Japan-exclusive. Fan outcry showed Nintendo that there was a big enough audience to justify a digital release, and the game was brought to America via the Wii U eShop.

## Related Appearances

Despite the game being absent in the West for decades, *Murasame*'s legacy can be seen in many titles published in America. The game's first appearance outside of Japan was in *Pikmin 2* for the Nintendo GameCube. The Cosmic Archive treasure is in fact a copy of the *Murasame Castle* disk.

The game also has a few connections with the *Super Smash Bros.* series. In *Brawl*, not only does Takamaru make an appearance as a sticker, but the *Murasame*'s musical theme can be unlocked for the classic Mario Bros. stage in *Brawl*.

You may also know that Takamaru makes an appearance within *Super Smash Bros.* for Wii U and 3DS as an Assist Trophy. But he was actually originally considered for the role of a playable fighter. This idea dates back to the development of *Super Smash Bros. Melee*. It's believed Takamaru's inclusion was scrapped due to his relatively obscure status. Masuhiro Sakurai, creator of the Smash Bros. series, stated that he was considered again for the fourth game in the series, but was again put aside because of a lack of popularity. Takamaru's appearance later inspired the design of the Mii Swordfighters, including his haircut and outfit.

Japan has also seen two more references that didn't make it to the West. Another Japan-exclusive title, which we covered in an earlier entry, is *Captain Rainbow*. Takamaru takes on a very prominent role within the game, appearing as an anxious young man who gets nervous around women.

*WarioWare: D.I.Y.* also includes a microgame exclusive to Japan. The player simply has to avoid shurikens from several ninjas while assuming the role of Takamaru. This was replaced in the West with a microgame based on *Pikmin* that plays entirely differently.

The Wii exclusive *Samurai Warriors 3* features a large reference to *Murasame* with the inclusion of the extra mode titled 'Murasame Castle mode'. This gives users the option of playing as Takamaru. By completing more of the main game, it also becomes possible to play as Takamaru within the game's other modes.

One of the more obscure pieces of media to come from the game was a TV drama produced in December of 1986. It was an adaptation of the game starring the cast of the all-girl pop group Onyanko Club for the TV series *Monday Drama Land*. The series was known for its adaptations of popular culture. Though clips of the episode have proven difficult to find, the episode was released on a DVD boxset in Japan.

# NAMCO X CAPCOM

**CONSOLE:** SONY PLAYSTATION 2
**YEAR:** 2005
**DEVELOPER:** MONOLITH SOFT
**PUBLISHER:** NAMCO
**REGION:** JAPAN

Capcom. Namco. Two of the biggest names in video game development, both have been around since the golden era of arcade games. Known for creating games where their characters cross over, the two companies have a history of not only competition but also cooperation. The first title in which both teams joined forces never made it to the West. Featuring a huge number of characters from both companies, that game is *Namco x Capcom*.

Developed by Monolith Soft, a subsidiary of Namco at the time, *Namco x Capcom* is a different take on the strategy RPG genre. To add in mechanics that both companies are known for, the game features a fighting side to it. Attacking enemies requires moving a unit into a position where they can reach the enemy. You are then able to initiate a fighting-style attack phase. This allows

players to attack the enemy with a variety of different moves by using the directional and circle buttons. You're given a limited number

**Dazz:**
This game is the reason I started the show *Region Locked*. At the time of *Namco x Capcom*'s release, my interest in the game was unparalleled by anything else, likely because of my ties to game sprites. Everything about the game seemed fresh and exciting, and my reaction to its lack of localisation was devastation. Learning that a team was even capable of making a fan translation for a PlayStation 2 game (a current generation console at the time!), I knew I had to play it. I imported the game, modded my console, and got onto playing. And I was disappointed. Because the game is incredibly repetitive, has a pretty poor plot, and doesn't really evolve as it progresses. That, however, doesn't diminish my love for the project, the translation, the cooperation of developers, and the sexy sprite work.

of attacks during this phase and must attempt to do as much damage as possible. Some attacks are stronger against some enemies compared to others. This is demonstrated through a menu prior to attacking the enemy that will tell you their weak points. The game rewards clever use of attacks to combo and air juggle, providing you with bonuses like additional attacks, stat boosts and damage modifiers. Performing all five different attacks during a battle will restore some of the unit's HP or MP, too. By building up enough attacks and filling a power gauge for your character, it's also possible to perform a strong special attack.

Some units are able to use special moves when two characters have an affinity with each other. For example, while some units move around as a pair, some are standalone characters that can be controlled on their own. Ryu and Ken are standalone units, but if both are close enough together they'll be able to team up for an attack that delivers even greater damage.

When it comes to an enemy unit attacking you, there are a few different defensive options. The normal option requires you to counter enemy moves by pressing directional buttons as they appear on screen. Successfully doing this will reward you with bonus AP and will make your character's turn

come quicker. You can even use some AP to absorb a portion of the damage dealt. There's also an option that will use up some of the character's special attack gauge in order to simply skip the fight and take the damage instead. Some characters have their own moves too, allowing them to counter attacks by using up some points from the power gauge. The game is very basic, with the main appeal of the title seeing beloved characters from your favourite series and how they'll crop up. Characters will know of each other, and common elements from each franchise will overlap to create a fully connected universe. This is done through dialogue, visual references, and elements you might not expect such as characters from different franchises teaming up for special attacks. This encourages players to explore character affinities and discover their Multiple Assault attacks.

The game's plot follows the characters of Reiji Arisu and Xiaomu in the year 20XX. The duo is tasked to investigate spiritual disturbances for a special underground organisation called Shinra. During the investigation, they discover quakes that are causing rifts to open between worlds, a disturbance that occurred ten years prior. These quakes cause several worlds to connect, and transport people between them. Heroes from all walks of gaming life are bundled together in your party, some from the biggest names in gaming and some from the smallest. The same is true of the villains of these games, who are working cooperatively against you.

A common complaint from reviewers was that fights become tedious after a few hours of playing and can distract from the plot. Maps often take over half an hour to complete, and there are a total of fifty throughout the game. Regarding how the game came into creation, Namco executive Yoichi Haraguchi stated prior to the game's release, 'Monolith Soft came to us, saying that they wanted to make a game that featured characters from Namco [...] Our company is celebrating its fiftieth anniversary in June, so we were thinking that it would be great to bring back our characters from the past.' The game had been a concept for two years until Namco came up with the idea of bringing in characters from another company. When thinking of developers they could work with, the only company Namco could think of with enough unique characters to match their own was Capcom. Keiji Inafune, who worked on the *Onimusha* and *Mega Man Legends* series for Capcom at the time, was extremely excited to see the game come to life. He stated, 'If it were a few years back, it would've been unthinkable to join hands with another rival company. But [companies] nowadays are more cooperative, and I think that it's a good thing for the video game industry. [...] I hope that we can collaborate together with Namco again in the future.'

*Namco x Capcom* led to several titles between both companies being released internationally. After this title came *Cross Edge*, an RPG released on the PlayStation 3 and Xbox 360 in 2008. The game was a collaboration between Namco, Capcom, Nippon Ichi and Gust. The two companies decided to then step away from RPGs and went for a genre they're both well known for: a fighting game that crossed over *Street Fighter* and *Tekken*.

Following that was the 3DS RPG *Project X Zone*, where not only are Namco and Capcom characters fighting together, but SEGA is thrown into the mix too. With the sequel *Project X Zone 2* being released, we also saw the introduction of Chrom and Lucina from *Fire Emblem: Awakening* joining the cast of playable characters, as well as Metal Face from *Xenoblade Chronicles* appearing as a rival. This meant that the game contained characters from not only Namco and Capcom, but SEGA and Nintendo as well.

## Localisation

We were unable to find an official statement on *Namco x Capcom*'s lack of localisation. Online sources cite various reasons, and we aren't able to confirm any of these. Some say that there were disputes between Namco and Capcom about who would be given the right to publish the game in the Western markets. Others believe that Namco didn't want to translate and publish the title outside of Japan because of the obscurity of many of the characters that appear within the game. A lot of the characters come from some very obscure titles that were also Japan exclusive. However, the characters of Reiji and Xiaomu did prove popular enough with Namco for them to be reused in later games.

A fan translation patch was created by the group TransGen. It translates a vast majority of the game into English, enough to push through the game's story and to get a handle on the battle system. Many believe the translation demonstrates the ability and determination of fans. While it might not be a perfect translation, and has a few minor spelling mistakes slipping in, it is still an admirable effort and one that should be seen as an inspiration.

# PANEKIT

**CONSOLE:** SONY PLAYSTATION
**YEAR:** 1999
**DEVELOPER:** SONY INTERACTIVE
**PUBLISHER:** SONY INTERACTIVE
**REGION:** JAPAN

When talking about open-world sandbox games, most will think of *Minecraft*, and the creative freedom it gives players. However, this concept isn't unique to *Minecraft*. One game with similar creative freedom was released exclusively in Japan, focusing primarily on creating interesting and unique vehicles. That game is *Panekit: Infinitive Crafting Toy Case*.

Panekit was developed and published by Sony Interactive in 1999 for the original PlayStation, preceding the likes of other vehicle-building games such as *Banjo Kazooie: Nuts & Bolts* and elements of *Garry's Mod*. *Panekit* is a sandbox game which allows the player to drive and create vehicles of their own imagination, with the intended audience being RC vehicle enthusiasts and model builders.

The range of customisation options in the game allow for a large number of different types of movement. While most navigation is made on land with vehicles that behave like

cars, some of the game's pre-built options demonstrate the variety that can be achieved.

The game has seven different types of panel that can be used for construction.

Core panels, which are the base of each model, becoming the central viewpoint for the game's camera. Standard panels, which are used for shaping the vehicle while also providing power; with each additional panel, more power is supplied. Joints, which can be assigned to button presses, bending parts of the vehicles by player-defined degrees of

---

**Dazz:**
*Panekit* is a game for very smart people. I am not a very smart person. Playing this game was a real struggle; I was able to use many of the vehicles provided by the game, but my ability to create my own was limited. I suspect that many engineers would make light work of the mental gymnastics I put myself through only to fail with each creation. It's a unique game, though I'd argue a remake would do it far more justice. If you get the chance to play it, I'd recommend it, but don't underestimate the trial and error of making a vehicle that will do your bidding.

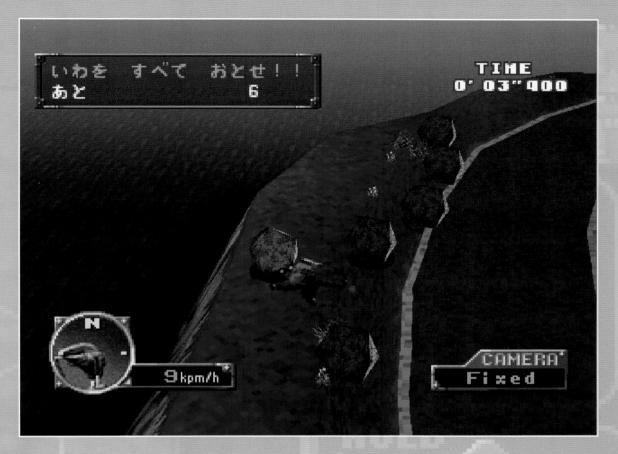

rotation. Tires, which serve the obvious task of letting a vehicle move along the ground with less resistance.

Motors, which rotate other panels — these can be used to create propellers for aerial movement, and by combining multiple motors together, it's possible to increase the amount of turning power. Jets, which provide propulsion and thrust. These use a large amount of power but can provide the most dramatic speeds and mobility. And finally, shooters, which give the vehicle a turret to shoot objects. By giving a turret full power levels, it will fire a laser with no recoil instead of bullets.

The game's vehicle editor may appear confusing at first, but the game includes a range of tutorials that show each step of the process with a voiceover. Another menu in

the editor can demonstrate exactly how the vehicle behaves, showing power distribution as well as visualising kinetic energy, helping the player to understand where drag and air resistance can cause issues. The game features PlayStation mouse support for the editor, making designing vehicles much quicker.

The player starts with a very basic car, which they can use to explore a small island. By completing missions provided through plinths or collecting chests, additional pre-designed vehicles can be unlocked, as well as bonus materials that can be used in builds. Certain tasks must be completed in order to unlock additional locations and vehicle build options, such as being able to get to the top of a hill, or destroying rocks which block paths.

Missions from plinths can vary dramatically, and may even require specific customisations to be made to the player's vehicle. These include races but can also include hurling a set number of rocks off a cliff, knocking balls into designated locations, or bowling. The game allows for fast travel between plinth markers.

*Panekit* released to very low sales figures; however, that didn't stop the game from seeing a digital rerelease on the Japanese PlayStation store in 2007. One of the key developers behind *Panekit*, Watanabe Kuniaki, tweeted in 2013 that the game had actually begun to make a profit as a result. Initially confused by the money coming in, he felt the need to confirm it with Sony, who told him that it wasn't a mistake; the game was finally making a profit.

Watanabe stated, 'During development, I've always said, "Let's make *Panekit* long and frugally," but the stock risk didn't allow it at the time. I never would've imagined for it to end up like this.' He also credits the game being featured on *Game Digging* for bringing more attention to the title, which is a show on the video sharing site Niconico.

Much of the game's appeal comes from its experimental nature, not just in what the game is, but in what the player can do. As each panel operates in a specific manner and cannot be improved on its own, combining panels into the best vehicle possible requires imagination and lateral thinking. *Panekit*'s online community is small, but the game has such open options that players have created unique and interesting builds, including recreating other vehicles from popular TV shows and media.

## Localisation

The game's low sales were very likely a contributing factor to the game's lack of localisation. With the game's main focus being critical thinking, its audience was limited, something which Sony probably considered. With the PlayStation 2 releasing only a few months after the game launched in Japan, it's possible that Sony also thought translation and distribution internationally would not be fruitful, as it could divert resources away from upcoming PlayStation 2 titles.

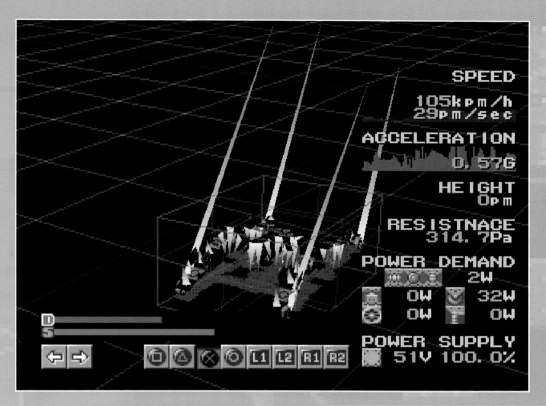

SPEED
105kpm/h
29pm/sec
ACCELERATION
0.57G
HEIGHT
0pm
RESISTNACE
314.7Pa
POWER DEMAND
2W
0W      32W
0W      0W
POWER SUPPLY
51V 100.0%

217kpm/h

CAMERA
Auto

# PINGU: THE MOST CHEERFUL PENGUIN IN THE WORLD

**CONSOLE:** NINTENDO GAME BOY
**YEAR:** 1993
**DEVELOPER:** TOM CREATE
**PUBLISHER:** BANDAI
**REGION:** JAPAN

It isn't rare to see a children's series take hold internationally, particularly if language isn't a major factor. This is why series like *Mr Bean*, a British show, can be appreciated regardless of whether you speak English or not. With the stop-motion series *Pingu*, all characters speak the made-up language of 'Pinguish'.

Initially created for a Swiss audience by Otmar Gutmann, the show was picked up by the BBC shortly after production began. *Pingu*'s popularity became strong worldwide, particularly in Japan; so much so that there's actually a Japanese-produced CGI *Pingu* series called *Pingu in the City*. Pingu's popularity in the region spawned many exclusive products and ventures, including a few video games produced by leading AAA developers.

*Pingu*'s first dip into the video game market came in 1993 on the Game Boy, with the release of the Japanese exclusive *Pingu: The Most Cheerful Penguin in the World*. Being one of the first games developed by 'Tom Create', the title was published by B-AI, a subsidiary of Bandai. The game lets the player live out Pingu's daily life. In a similar fashion to the television show, each level has Pingu perform different activities, with four levels in total.

In Level 1, having eaten all of the one fish in the igloo, Pingu is instructed to go out and catch ten more. To do so, the player attaches bait to the line and lowers it down. Once a fish is hooked, they must then hit the A button as quickly as possible to bring the fish up to the surface.

In Level 2, Pingu takes his younger sister Pinga out, but as soon as he turns his back, she becomes stranded on a floating block of ice. Pingu must then jump between moving platforms to reach his sister.

> **Greg:**
> The Game Boy game is too easy for such a short game, aside from one frustrating platforming game. Probably a game for small children.

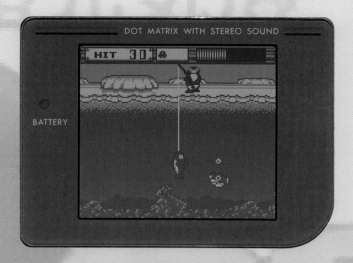

Level 3 sees Pingu accidentally breaking a vase. In an attempt to replace it, he goes to the shop which has only a single vase for sale. The shopkeeper asks for a fish in return. Forgetting his fishing abilities from Level 1, Pingu must score three points against each member of an ice hockey team one by one in order to win a fish.

For Level 4, we see Pingu bored and seeking attention from his mother. Busy with Pinga, she tells him to go and find something to do. Whilst wandering outside, Pingu comes across some other penguins having a snowball fight. Pingu must then defeat them in three increasingly difficult rounds to win the game.

Additional minigames can be unlocked by exploring the many igloos around Pingu's home, such as a sliding image puzzle, or a simple clone of *Puyo Puyo*. A number of Easter eggs are also hidden in the title through the game's password screen. The password 'Pingu, Snowman, Dad, Mum' reveals a looping animation of Pingu dancing. 'Pingu, Robby, Pinga, Snowman' displays an image of Pingu and Pinga. And entering 'Pingu, Dad, Mum, Pinga' will grant the player access to a sound test menu.

# FUN! FUN! PINGU ~ WELCOME! TO ANTARCTICA ~

**CONSOLE:**     SONY PLAYSTATION
**YEAR:**        1999
**DEVELOPER:**   C-LAB
**PUBLISHER:**   SONY MUSIC ENTERTAINMENT
**REGION:**      JAPAN

The second Japanese exclusive Pingu game is *Fun! Fun! Pingu ~ Welcome! To Antarctica ~*, developed by C-Lab and published by Sony Music Entertainment for the original PlayStation. Similar to his first outing on the Game Boy, this release once again sees Pingu exploring his home and playing through various minigames. More complex than earlier *Pingu* releases, the player is given control over how they interact with scenery between minigames. Pingu can run, speak with other characters, and has dedicated buttons for its signature 'nooting' both forward and above.

The main focus of the game is to complete requests for people around Pingu's home while listening to repeating fifteen-second samples of music. Each chapter focuses on different problems that must be solved. Usually, these involve Pingu travelling to a location, picking up an item and using that item to progress through the game. To complete each level the player must also beat a minigame relating to the objective.

After each minigame is unlocked, it can then be replayed from the game's main menu. The team that worked on the *Pingu*

TV show, Pygos Group, assisted with the creation of Pingu's first 3D adventure. This would also be the only time that a character would be introduced in a *Pingu* game, Popoff, though he doesn't make any appearances outside of this title.

> **Greg:**
> The PlayStation game is aggressively slow, painfully dull, way too easy and just not fun. Probably a game for small children.

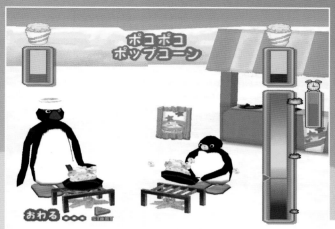

# PINGU'S WONDERFUL CARNIVAL!

**CONSOLE:** NINTENDO DS
**YEAR:** 2008
**DEVELOPER:** SQUARE ENIX
**PUBLISHER:** SQUARE ENIX
**REGION:** JAPAN

The next Japanese exclusive *Pingu* game we'll be talking about was developed and published by Square Enix: *Pingu's Wonderful Carnival!*, which was released on the Nintendo DS in 2008. Once again, the game is formed of several minigames starring Pingu and his family. By exploring the world with the game's touch screen, Pingu will meet a number of characters who host various minigames. As we've seen from the earlier *Pingu* releases, these games range from simplistic fishing, cleaning the family home while preventing Pinga from causing more mess, and *Cooking Mama* style cooking games. By completing a range of objectives, the player is rewarded with items and money which can be spent on customisation options such as hats.

## Localisation

These three games never saw a release outside of Japan. While no specifics can be given as to why this is, complications with games following international franchises are, as we often say, nothing new. It's clear that the team behind *Pingu* saw promise in the Japanese region. Not only did the franchise have three exclusive games in Japan, but

the region also had a series of PlayStation gamepads designed for children's hands with smaller grips, and various figures of characters on top of them.

The 2008 release of *Pingu's Wonderful Carnival!* on the Nintendo DS came after Square Enix announced plans to expand its operations. They created the Pure Dreams brand, focusing on character franchises. *Pingu* was the first in their launch lineup for this project, followed by a game based on Snoopy. These seem to be the only two games created for Pure Dreams, so it's likely the venture wasn't as fruitful as Square Enix had hoped, and doubt was cast upon how successful the titles would be overseas.

Greg:
The DS game is the best of a bad bunch. But the games are too easy.
Probably a game for small children.
In summary, I think these might be games for small children.

# POKÉMON: CARD GB2

**CONSOLE:** NINTENDO GAME BOY
**YEAR:** 2001
**DEVELOPER:** HUDSON SOFT
**PUBLISHER:** NINTENDO
**REGION:** JAPAN

Software that isn't published in the US tends to be part of an obscure franchise, but this title comes from one of gaming's best-known series: Pokémon. The Pokémon franchise exploded during the 1990s. As with most popular series, Pokémon's creators tried to capitalise on the success of the anime and video games by creating a trading card game. Since the first generation of Pokémon had already established a battle system, the trading card game's rules took inspiration from the Game Boy games. The card game launched in Japan in 1996, and reached the United States around two and a half years later. It took America by storm and became a trend amongst the nation's kids.

During this two-and-a-half-year gap, a brand-new Pokémon game was released in Japan based on the trading cards. A year after this game came out in its home country, it was translated and published in the West as *Pokémon Trading Card Game* for the Game Boy. Due to the success of the game, a second title was created and released in Japan in 2001. Although many Western fans waited for the second game

to be localised, it never made it to the West. Before we get into the details of the second game, we're going to talk a little about the first game.

Just as the actual card game took inspiration from the original Pokémon games, so does the trading card video game. The player collects a deck of cards from a professor based on the elements of fire, water or grass. They must compete against various characters in the world. This includes a rival, eight club leaders based on different elemental types, and four card player grand masters. The player can also create their own deck with cards obtained throughout the game and can save the various decks using computers.

Although it borrowed many elements from the original games, the *Pokémon Trading Card Game* also introduced ideas

that became a standard for the series. One example is the ability to run by holding in the B button. This was introduced to the core series in *Pokémon Ruby* and *Sapphire*, but until the trading card game, no such ability existed in the series.

The game featured digitised versions of real cards that were illustrated by Ken Sugimori, Mitsuhiro Arita and Keiji Kinebuchi. There is a total of 228 cards featured in the title, but some of these cards couldn't be obtained without the use of the Card Pop! feature. Card Pop! allowed two players to link up their games using the Game Boy Color's infrared function, which would provide both players with a random card, similar to the Mystery Gift system found within the core titles.

The title was created by Hudson Soft, and originally announced under the name *Pokémon Card*. The project's Western release was initially delayed by two months; it's believed this was done so Nintendo could focus their marketing on *Pokémon Stadium* for the Nintendo 64.

When the game was released, it came with a promotional card featuring Meowth. This card was only available with the game and wasn't sold anywhere else in the West. In Japan, a special legendary Dragonite was given away instead, which was made exclusive to the region. While most cards appeared within the title, two were missing: Electrode from the Base Set and Ditto from the Fossil Set. This was due to difficulties getting their abilities to work within the game's engine. As a result, a new card for each Pokémon was made exclusively for the game. The Electrode card, however, was later made available from an online card shop.

The game features two cameo appearances in the characters of Mr Ishihara and Imakuni?. These are both the president and CEO of The Pokémon Company, Tsunekazu Ishihara, and *Pokémon* anime musician Tomoaki Imakuni. Imakuni's appearance with a question mark resembles that of his stage name.

*Pokémon Trading Card Game* was praised and had successful sales. Over 600,000 copies were sold in Japan by the end of 1999, and around 1.5 million copies were sold in America in its first year.

With the growing popularity of the trading card game, it seemed inevitable that there would be a sequel. With several expansions to the physical card game being made, there was plenty of content to use for another game.

Also developed by Hudson, the sequel was titled *Pokémon Card GB2: Here Comes Team GR!* The game boasted several new features and improvements over the previous title. This included being able to choose your gender, an extensive training mode to educate new players, and a diagnosis system that let the player know how effective their deck was.

Many new cards had been published since the first game was released. These additional cards were added to the game, bringing its total up to 445. While this number is higher than the original, a large number of cards were left out.

The game's story was also expanded and didn't simply revolve around the player collecting club medals and defeating the Grand Masters. A new rival team appears called Team Great Rocket. Led by King Biruritchi, the team kidnapped a number of Club Masters and stole almost everybody's Pokémon cards. It's the player's role to save the Club Masters and defeat Team Great Rocket in their HQ.

As a direct sequel, the game not only allows the player to explore the island found in the first *Trading Card Game*, but also a second island called GR Island. This makes

the game's world seem much more fleshed out and improves upon the relatively short length of the first game.

New graphical features were added too. Opponents now have a variety of expressions after a duel commences, such as being happy when winning or sad when losing. Another change is the introduction of coins. These coins are awarded after winning a club match, as opposed to the medals found in the first game. They can even be used to replace the coin during coin flips throughout the game.

A noticeable difference between the two games is in how the entranceway of each gym is presented. Originally, each gym only had a different symbol to define it. In the second game the entire room is themed after the gym's elemental type.

Another new feature is a game centre, which features several minigames. These include a game where the player has to flip and land a coin on heads over and over again. Doing this ten times unlocks a Mew card. There are also slot machines, which have a bonus game attached. Unlike in the core series, the slot machine plays itself, and has no user input for stopping the reels. These minigames grant tokens to the player

that could be traded for additional cards.

While the previous game featured connectivity through the use of the Game Boy's link cable, it isn't possible to connect the original trading card game to the sequel. Battles and trading between generations was a highly praised feature of the core series Game Boy games, and was expected to be in the second card game too. As a result, when players tried to perform a Card Pop! between the first and second card games, several issues occurred. This included glitches like the games freezing, or data from the first game being completely lost.

The Card Pop! was again one of the only ways of obtaining two cards within the game: Lugia and Here Comes Team Rocket! Similar to the previous title, a trading card was made to promote the game: Great Rocket's Mewtwo. The card was planned to be bundled with the game but was packaged with the special edition Celebi Game Boy Advance instead for unknown reasons.

## Localisation

*Pokémon Card GB2* wasn't released in Japan until 28 March 2001, which was a week after the launch of the Game Boy Advance. This was problematic for the original Game Boy as a platform, as the introduction of new hardware usually means the death of the previous device. The first trading card video game took years to be localised, and the sequel was literally twice its size. The Game Boy Advance was released in North America just three months after it came out in Japan. So even if the game had been localised at breakneck speed and only took around a year to come to the West, it would have been published on a dying platform.

Although the game would likely have seen respectable sales figures, Nintendo probably cut their losses in order to focus on the development and marketing of new Game Boy Advance games. The success of their new hardware would have been far more important to them than the success of a single game. If a console doesn't sell well at launch, it may lack support from other companies. And a lack of games could trigger a snowball effect of poorer and poorer sales on the platform.

Footnote: special thanks to Artemis251 for his work on an English fan translation patch.

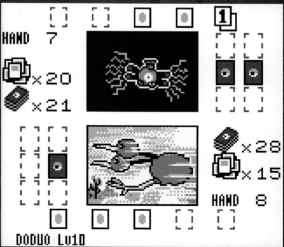

# POLICENAUTS

**CONSOLE:** NEC PC-9821, PANASONIC 3DO, SONY PLAYSTATION, SEGA SATURN

**YEAR:** 1994 (NEC), 1995 (3DO), 1996 (PS, SATURN)

**DEVELOPER:** KONAMI

**PUBLISHER:** KONAMI

**REGION:** JAPAN

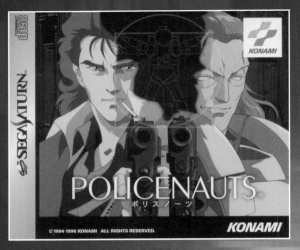

Hideo Kojima is one of the few video game designers that needs no introduction. With his rich plethora of games from *Zone of the Enders* to *Death Stranding* and of course his *Metal Gear* series, fans have collected, obsessed over and attempted to play every game that has his name attached. This hasn't been a problem as all his games have been released and translated outside of Japan with the exception of one. *Policenauts* was released in 1994 for the NEC PC-9821, with a Panasonic 3DO port a year later, and a release on the PlayStation and SEGA Saturn in 1996. Most people consider the SEGA Saturn release the definitive version for its updated visuals, light gun support, and the inclusion of bonus content.

    *Policenauts* has a crime noir cyberpunk

**Matt Barnes:**

My main reason to play *Policenauts* was because it made no sense that it had Meryl Silverburgh in it. I (and everyone else) have been obsessed with *Metal Gear Solid* since the PlayStation 1 days, researching everything associated with it. Many years later I finally got to play, and it didn't disappoint. It surprised me in so many ways. A serious noir point and click with an engaging story (though the pacing is now a tad slow). The visuals and the soundtrack? Well they are exceptional. In so many cases it suffers from its time (boob physics) but like most games by Hideo Kojima it is still a high-quality game to play and I believe it would have become a cult classic in the West if it had been released over here.

aesthetic, taking inspiration from films such as *Blade Runner* and *Lethal Weapon*. The game follows the story of Jonathan Ingram, a member of the *Policenauts*, a group of five astronauts with extensive police training who are assigned to protect Beyond Coast, the first functioning space colony in the year 2013.

While he is testing a new spacesuit, an accident causes Jonathan to drift from his craft into deep space. Though presumed dead by his team, Jonathan survived the incident with the assistance of a deep-sleep module built into his suit, leaving him in a deep slumber for twenty-four years, waking in the year 2037. Three years after his rescue, Jonathan, who has taken up the profession of a private detective in Old Los Angeles, is visited by his ex-wife, Lorraine. She asks Jonathan to assist in solving the case of her missing husband, Kenzo Hojo. The only clues to his whereabouts are a torn leaf, a small collection of pills, and the word 'Plato'.

After leaving Jonathan's office, Lorraine is murdered by a man wearing a motorcycle helmet. Unable to catch the assailant, and despite his initial reluctance, Jonathan decides to take on her final request.

Jonathan travels to Beyond, reuniting with his old partner from the LAPD, Ed Brown. The two set out to investigate the suspicious circumstances surrounding both Hojo's disappearance and Lorraine's murder.

While primarily a graphic adventure game, *Policenauts* also includes puzzle solving and even shooting. With the game's Saturn release, new features were added to allow the player to use the console's 'Virtua Gun', known as the 'Stunner' in North America, and play these sections as a light gun shooter. The game features a

Top image: NEC PC-9801; bottom image: SEGA Saturn

brief bomb disposal section and other small asides to the main game.

When it comes to investigation, the player is able to inspect objects and question characters multiple times in order to uncover additional information, opening extra dialogue and descriptions. This is a necessity as often the game restricts progress unless the player probes for more information or investigates all elements of a scene.

With certain choices changing the tones and mood of characters, the player's actions can alter the responses they get. This opens the possibility for multiple ways of progressing through the game.

Hideo Kojima's classic style is obviously present throughout the game with its film-like cutscenes, extensive dialogue and tendency to break the fourth wall. *Policenauts* is the first of his games to include Summary Screens, which remind the player of the plot when

loading a save file. It is also the first time he introduces each of the key characters with their name and the voice actor who plays them. Hideo Kojima explained how *Policenauts* came to be in an interview with the *Guardian*. While working on *Metal Gear* and *Metal Gear 2* Kojima expressed there was a difficulty asking programmers to implement very specific dialogue or music cues because he found that they would work to their own style or timing. He stated, 'It was hugely frustrating making games at that time for me. I wanted to control everything. So, after the second *Metal Gear* launched, I developed my own scripting engine and decided to work on adventure games so that I could have complete control over when the animation played or when the music triggered. That's when I developed *Snatcher* and *Policenauts*. It was a way to take creative control back from the programmers.'

Karen's sick. You have to help her.

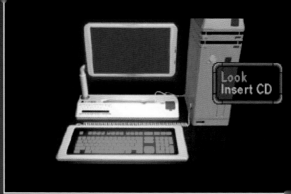

Look
Insert CD

Initially conceived under the title *Beyond*, the game became *Policenauts* because Konami were unable to claim a copyright on just a single standard word. The game was also originally going to be listed under the new genre of 'Cinematic Virtual Reality'; this had to be changed to 'Interactive Cinema', however, as the term 'Virtual Reality' had already been trademarked. Four Japanese voice artists went on to have roles in *Metal Gear Solid* on the PlayStation 1. Hideyuki Tanaka, the voice of Jonathan Ingram in *Policenauts*, also voiced Hal Emmerich or Otacon. Kaneto Shiozawa, who plays Tony Redwood, voiced Gray Fox. Naoko Nakamura plays the BCCH receptionist and played Sniper Wolf, and lastly Masaharu Satō, who played Salvatore Toscanini, featured as Donald Anderson in *Metal Gear Solid*.

However, it wasn't just voice actors that Kojima carried over into the *Metal Gear Solid* series. A sample of the 'End of the Dark' track from the *Policenauts* soundtrack is played over the Konami Computer Entertainment logo screen in *Metal Gear Solid*. Meryl Silverburgh also features in the game as part of 'Vice Unit'. Though she isn't actually the same character that's featured in *Metal Gear Solid*, she has a very similar appearance and she was the last member of FOXHOUND before it was disbanded after the fall of Zanzibar Land. Incidentally, *Metal*

*Gear Solid 4* also references Vice Unit by having Meryl wear a bullet earring like she does in *Policenauts*, and the Rat Patrol Team 01 consists of Jonathan and Ed in reference to the main characters Jonathan Ingram and the chief of Vice Ed Brown, who themselves appear to be inspired by Riggs and Murtaugh from the *Lethal Weapon* series of films. Meryl also wears Dave Forrest's orange jacket in the end scene of *Metal Gear Solid*, at the same time as Solid Snake also reveals his name to be David. In Metal Gear Solid 4, Drebin 893's favourite soda is Narc, the same name as the addictive drug in *Policenauts*. Otacon seems to be a big fan of *Policenauts*. In *Metal Gear Solid* he has posters of the game on his wall and it's even visually referenced when discussing Bipedal Tanks, and in *Metal Gear Solid 4* it's Otacon's PC desktop wallpaper on the *Nomad*. The exoskeletons worn by the various ninjas throughout the *Metal Gear Solid* series are made by Tokugawa Heavy Industries, a company featured in *Policenauts*. These are just a few of the references Kojima has included in the *Metal Gear Solid* series. Kojima also lent his own voice to the game in a brief cameo as an AP officer in the shootout at Tokugawa Heavy Industries.

The game also includes references to other titles published by Konami, such as a shelf of CDs containing musical tracks from different games. While this area is only a minor part of the overall release, it actually takes up a large amount of the game's disc space, totalling a sixth of the game's overall size. When it came to producing the game, concerns were raised about how much could ultimately be included, with this section being considered the easiest to cut back should storage issues arise. In the opening cutscene of the game, a neon sign can be seen in the background of one of the images that reads 'Solid Snake'. Even Jonathan Ingram's surname could be a reference to the Ingram MAC-11, the sub machine gun that featured in both *Metal Gear* and *Metal Gear 2*. There are also several references to Kojima's previous adventure game, *Snatcher*. In the Ishidas' pharmacy, the player can see the *Snatcher* calendar hanging on the end of a row of shelves. A message on Jonathan's answering machine plays the music from the club Outer Heaven in *Snatcher*. A newspaper article on Jonathan's wall is from the *Neo Kobe Newspaper*; Neo Kobe is the fictional city in which *Snatcher* takes place. In the game *Tokimeki Memorial*, which was also produced by Hideo Kojima, it is possible to watch a 'movie' of *Policenauts*. Again, there are plenty more references throughout the game; these are just some of the least obscure.

The initial NEC PC release is the only version to feature the hand-drawn pixel art, as the computer rendered all of the graphics in real time. These graphics were completely overhauled for the 3DO release of the game and all subsequent releases. The special edition of the 3DO version came bundled with a mouse and official *Policenauts* mouse mat. Shortly before this release, Konami put out a demo in the form of a 'pilot disk'. The disk also contained various interviews with voice actors and developers and

even an in-depth encyclopedia about the world of *Policenauts*. Some of this information came included as extra content in both the PlayStation and Saturn versions. Other than the light-gun support for the Saturn and the increase in framerate of the cutscenes to 24fps from the PlayStation's 15fps, there are few differences between these final releases of the game. Hideo Kojima opposed one change in particular relating to the player's ability to jiggle women's breasts, as Shuhei Yoshida, the CEO of Sony Interactive Entertainment, found it excessive. Kojima recalled this in an interview with Famitsu: 'I was contacted by [Sony Computer Entertainment], who told me, "We're going to decide in an upcoming meeting how many times breasts can jiggle." I argued over and over with them, saying, "That's absurd!" [...] In the end, we worked things out, but I'll never forget arguing over the "breast jiggle issue".' In the PlayStation version of the game, the animation of the jiggling was reduced and the player also had fewer opportunities to do it.

## Localisation

While *Policenauts* never received an official English release, there was a time when a release overseas was considered. This is confirmed by the presence of an English press release on Konami's official website in 1996, claiming the game to be a sequel to Kojima's *Snatcher* on the SEGA Saturn. The game also had an English mock-up cover shot produced and printed in several promotional pamphlets for SEGA games, packed with other Saturn titles.

However, according to translator Jeremy Blaustein, who had worked on the official translations of both *Snatcher* and *Metal Gear Solid*, rumours of an official partially completed *Policenauts* translation script are false. He said, 'It is false as far as I know. I was in the international business department at Konami when it came out and I never heard of any plans to release in the US, then or since.'

Contradicting this, according to Kojima, the international version was worked on, but the developers weren't able to sync the game's English dialogue with the animated cutscenes, though the legitimacy of this claim cannot be confirmed. The game never saw a North American release, and in the end it would be up to fans to create their own translations, the first of which was the PlayStation version of the game. The project had a long development period, with Marc Laidlaw (not to be confused with the writer for *Half-Life*) and Artemio Urbina translating much of the dialogue in the summer of 2007, but encountering problems when it came to programming their translation into the game itself. It would be a year before Something Awful forum user 'slowbeef' began work on

getting the script inserted into the game, leading a revival of the project which would come to completion in 2009.

Despite the PlayStation version being considered an inferior release to the Saturn's, it would be a number of years before another translation would surface for the SEGA console, once again built upon translation work from Marc Laidlaw.

# RAKUGAKIDS

**CONSOLE:** NINTENDO 64
**YEAR:** 1998
**DEVELOPER:** KONAMI
**PUBLISHER:** KONAMI
**REGION:** JAPAN AND EUROPE

*Rakugakids* is an interesting take on the fighting genre, appearing on a console with a distinct shortage of exclusive fighting games, the Nintendo 64. Created in 1998 by Konami, *Rakugakids* is a straightforward fighting game that has the player take on the role of various children and the characters they've created.

The game's title is a play on the word Rakugaki, a Japanese term effectively meaning 'doodle'. This is fitting, as the game's use of doodle-like artwork and childish character design plays into this theme. The game's story follows six children who discover some magical crayons in a cave. The kids decide to share the eight crayons between themselves, but the remaining two crayons and their box are stolen by the local neighbourhood bully. The kids discover that anything drawn with these crayons comes to life, so in order to get them back, they decide to draw their way to victory.

These heroes include: Andy and his drawing Astronots, a spaceman who takes

the role of the game's frontman; DDJ and Captain.Cat.Kit, a breakdancing cat that attacks its opponent with music; Nola and Marsa, a witch that wears a chicken hat and has the ability to jump huge distances; Jerry and Robot C.H.O., a bot who may be slow, but is capable of dealing massive damage; Clione and Beartank, a teddy bear with a tank turret and treads who is always tired; Roy and Cools. Roy, a cowboy who plays similarly to Astronots. There's also Val and Mamezo, a monster capable of morphing into various different forms like scissors, an iron or a spoon...

In a typical style of its time, the game makes use of flat characters on a 3D plane, not unlike *PaRappa the Rapper* or Nintendo's *Paper Mario*. The title plays similarly to other fighting games,

---

**Dazz:**
I used to own this game as a kid and had absolutely no idea it was never released in the United States. I saw it as a classic of the Nintendo 64, one which many who owned the console would know of, as I also knew Konami would continually use Beartank in future games too. *Rakugakids* isn't a great fighting game, but it definitely has an interesting style.

with attacks and combos being performed with the directional and attack buttons. Each fighter is capable of double jumping, and there are three punch buttons and three kick buttons, alongside a taunt, and a button used to perform 'magic' attacks. These magic attacks allow the player to perform three strong moves after their super bar fills at the bottom of the screen. These are performed by pressing the magic button and holding in different directions.

The three types of magical combat include 'Attack Magic', a move capable of dealing a large quantity of damage; 'Defence Magic', a move which has the potential to put some distance between the players so they can re-evaluate their tactics; and 'Counterattack Magic' which is performed while the opponent is blocking, and can inflict a decent amount of damage as well as giving the player some space. An interesting mode in the game comes in the form of Training Mode, a way of training a character to play through the game for you. This mode has the player select a character, train them by competing against other characters, and having them become better at fighting. The game is programmed to learn your play style, allowing you to set your character to automatically work through the game's story mode without your input.

The reception of *Rakugakids* was somewhat positive, with many praising its unique art style, though complaints regularly included issues with 'flow'. Attacks feel quite stiff and restricted, and with the game's variety of characters it can often be hard to work out how to go about attacking your opponent. Many also showed distaste towards the game's loading screens, not understanding why they should need to exist on a cartridge-based title. The reasons behind these loading screens is likely due to the game's most praised feature: its artwork. Each character has an incredibly large number of frames, all of which need to be loaded into the Nintendo 64's 4MB of RAM.

Koji Yoshida, the game's director, had previously worked on *Street Fighter II* as a software designer, and *Final Fight* as a programmer. After *Rakugakids*, he would go on to work on a number of other notable projects, such as directing *Goemon: Mononoke Sugoroku*, and programming *Castlevania: Circle of the Moon* and *The Legend of Zelda: Oracle of Ages* and *Seasons*.

Several references to *Rakugakids* can be found within Yoshida's other works. These include unlikely appearances, such as in his work on *Circle of the Moon*. Nathan is capable of transforming into Clione's

drawing Beartank by equipping the Bear Ring and activating the Black Dog and Pluto cards. Rather than turn into a skeleton, as normally happens with using these cards, the player is instead turned into the sleepy teddy bear, capable of firing projectiles. Beartank has a high level of attack but suffers from the hindrance of dying from a single blow.

Beartank proved to be a popular character within Konami, later going on to appear as a playable character in Konami's kart racer, *Konami Krazy Racers*, alongside several other popular Konami characters.

## Localisation

*Rakugakids* never received a US release, only being published in Japan and Europe. The reasons behind this aren't fully known. Since the game had a European release, there *was* an English translation already made. The Nintendo 64 was prolific with its expansive library of child-friendly titles, and *Rakugakids*' art style fits this theme well. *Rakugakids* was released in 1998, the same year as Marvel vs. Capcom's *X-Men vs. Street Fighter*, and only a single year after *Tekken 3*. This is a period in console gaming history when fighting games were fairly common, so it's possible that *Rakugakids*, for all of its positive feedback,

was deemed mediocre when compared to the AAA fighting games of the time. With this in mind, Konami may have refrained from publishing the title in the US, knowing that the competition was too strong, and that the market for a child-friendly fighting game may not be too big.

# REAL SOUND: KAZE NO REGRET

**CONSOLE:** SEGA SATURN, SEGA DREAMCAST

**YEAR:** 1997 (SATURN), 1999 (DREAMCAST)

**DEVELOPER:** WARP, INC.

**PUBLISHER:** SEGA

**REGION:** JAPAN

Video games by their nature involve a lot of emphasis on visualisation. A trend with developers of late has been to improve accessibility of their titles through optional tweaks, such as button reassignment to assist those with limited use of their hands, as well as colour-blind modes which help differentiate objects in more ways than just their colours.

But what about those hindered by a lack of sight? For the Japanese, they had *Real Sound: Kaze no Regret*.

*Real Sound: Kaze no Regret* was developed by WARP, Inc. and published by SEGA in 1997 for the SEGA Saturn, with a rerelease on the Dreamcast in 1999. Unlike 99% of video games, *Real Sound* involved almost no video element.

The game's Dreamcast rerelease did feature an optional 'visual mode', but the main focus was of course on the game's audio, so it would only display photographs of little relevance while the game is played.

Taking the form of a radio drama, the game will play audio tracks of the game's plot, with chimes coming in when the player is required to make a choice moving forward, similar to visual novels or physical gamebooks.

The game follows a story unfolding in Tokyo. Izumi Sakurai has moved to a new elementary school and she joins a new class. She is seated next to Hiroshi Nonomura, and the two begin to fall in love. This love leads them to the decision to run away together, but when it comes to the arranged time to meet at the clock tower to leave together, Izumi doesn't show up. Shortly thereafter, she is transferred to a new school...

**Matt Barnes:**
I'm so glad we could get this information out in this book. We had an idea of doing a video by changing background images to random pictures as a sort of homage to the Dreamcast port, but in the end a video would have been too difficult to make. This is the only game we haven't been able to play, for obvious reasons. But I still think it would be fun if there was a way of getting some good actors together and dubbing this game, just to experience it, as it would have been for Western audiences.

*Real Sound* was created with the sole intention of giving gaming access to a whole new market who were mostly ignored previously: the blind. President of WARP, Inc., Kenji Eno, had previously created *D*, a horror-themed adventure game that acted as a sort of interactive film. After receiving a number of letters from fans of his games suffering from blindness, he visited several of those who contacted him so that he could learn more about how they had played his other titles.

In an interview with 1Up in 2008, Eno described how he saw *Real Sound* as a means to increasing accessibility with players in more ways than just how the player interacts with the game itself:

'Of course, [blind people are] not able to have the full experience, and they're kind of trying to force themselves to be able

to play, but they're making the effort. So I thought that if you turn off the monitor, both of you are just hearing the game. So after you finish the game, you can have an equal conversation about it with a blind person. That's an inspiration behind [*Real Sound: Kaze no Regret*] as well.'

In an agreement with SEGA, Eno gave the company exclusive rights to the title. In exchange, SEGA donated 1,000 SEGA Saturn consoles to the blind, with Eno sweetening the donation by providing 1,000 copies of the game to go with them.

While the game could very easily be ported and rereleased, sadly Eno passed away in 2013. Eno gave all rights over the title to SEGA, so the effort would need to come from within the company.

It's believed that WARP's creation of an audio-focused game inspired elements of

their future titles, such as *Enemy Zero*, in which enemies would be invisible and only found through sound cues, as well as *D2*, where sensory limitations are applied to the character including being blind or deaf at certain portions of the story.

## Localisation

*Real Sound* has a multitude of strong reasons for not receiving an international release; the game is entirely played through audio, so any translation would require an entire cast of voice actors for whichever language the game is to be released. With the main demographic those with visual impairment, players are limited, as this is a market often ignored by the games industry. During the time of the game's release, accessibility was not yet a major interest to game developers, though now there are full job roles designed specifically with this idea in mind.

Plans were made for two more sightless-friendly games to make *Real Sound* into a series, with each entry concentrating on entirely different themes and plot. The first was *Kiri no Oregel*, meaning 'Organ of the Fog', a horror game which even received advertisements in several magazines. The title was ultimately cancelled, with the reason cited being issues with audio compression for the game's voice tracks. A number of story elements from this title were later used in *D2*.

The third release would have been *Spy Lunch*, a comedy game which didn't really get far into development and never saw much in the way of public attention.

Because of *Real Sound*'s limited market, the game sold poorly. The game has become a highly sought-after collectible, thanks to the physical items provided alongside the software, such as instructions in Braille and, oddly, a bag of seeds.

# BS THE LEGEND OF ZELDA

| CONSOLE: | SUPER FAMICOM (BROADCAST SATELLAVIEW) |
|---|---|
| YEAR: | 1995/1996 |
| DEVELOPER: | NINTENDO, NINTENDO RESEARCH & DEVELOPMENT NO. 2 |
| PUBLISHER: | ST.GIGA |
| REGION: | JAPAN |

# BS THE LEGEND OF ZELDA: ANCIENT STONE TABLETS

| CONSOLE: | SUPER FAMICOM (BROADCAST SATELLAVIEW) |
|---|---|
| YEAR: | 1997 |
| DEVELOPER: | NINTENDO, NINTENDO RESEARCH & DEVELOPMENT NO. 2 |
| PUBLISHER: | ST.GIGA |
| REGION: | JAPAN |

The Satellaview was released exclusively in Japan in 1995, allowing users to connect to a digital satellite and stream data to their console. This worked in a similar fashion to the Internet services commonly seen today, allowing players to read magazines, add additional content to existing games, and even download new games to a memory pack. These streams would have a designated time of broadcast and cut-off time. The Satellaview's games were also usually prefixed with the letters 'BS', an abbreviation of the term Broadcast Satellaview.

Two *Zelda* titles were never rereleased, and as a result are only playable thanks to a dedicated fan community. We'll start with a look at *BS The Legend of Zelda*.

*BS Zelda* is a fully-fledged remake of the original *Legend of Zelda* published on the NES in 1986. With *BS Zelda* being on the Super Nintendo, the game's graphics were recreated within 16-bit limitations. The title plays in the same fashion as the game's original release with a few changes, both minor and major. Examples are that the Super Nintendo's L and R buttons allow the player to switch between items on the fly, and the maximum number of rupees is increased from 255 to 999.

Alterations were also made to the game's map, reducing the game's overworld as well as completely changing the layouts of the dungeons. These changes have caused many fans to refer to the title as a 'Third Quest' for *The Legend of Zelda*, as the original had a Second Quest that was unlocked after beating the game. A feature that couldn't be done without the Satellaview was the game's use of the SoundLink system, allowing a narrator to provide hints and tips at certain points of the live stream. This narrator is alleged to be the old man from the start of the game.

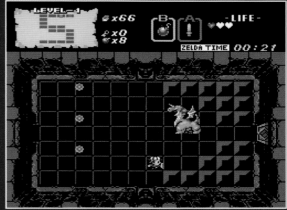

Two versions of *BS Zelda* were broadcast. Between 9 August and 30 August 1995, the version known as the Third Quest was streamed to the console. However, in December of 1996, a version featuring a different world was broadcast. This is often referred to as the 'Map 2' version of the game, or the Fourth Quest. Because the game was streamed to players, it had to be played in real time. As a result, events would occur at certain points during a broadcast, such as killing all enemies on screen, or giving the player an unlimited quantity of items. The game was streamed in four weekly instalments, and players had to tune in at those times if they wanted to play.

Another feature of the broadcast is that the player is actually not taking control of Link. Instead, the title makes use of the Satellaview's mascots. These are a red-headed girl and a boy with a baseball cap. The player's name and gender were determined by the user's settings on the BS-X hardware and loaded into the game. This is the first time a Nintendo-developed *Zelda* game would feature a female protagonist. Prior to this release, the only *Zelda* games to have a playable female character were the CD-i titles by Philips. This playable character is known as the Hero of Light, a character that would be explored

more in the next game we'll be looking at: *BS The Legend of Zelda: Ancient Stone Tablets*.

Broadcast in 1997, *BS The Legend of Zelda: Ancient Stone Tablets* made use of the Super Nintendo's *Link to the Past* engine, once again putting the player in the shoes of the Hero of Light. A number of changes were made to the game's mechanics, such as being able to switch direction while using the Pegasus Boots. This was possibly inspired by the ability to change direction while running in *Marvelous: Another Treasure Island* by Eiji Aonuma. The title is often seen as a sort of Second Quest for *A Link to the Past*, as many elements from the original game are reused and rearranged to create an original release. The difference to most standard Second Quests within the *Zelda* series is that *Ancient Stone Tablets* actually features its own unique storyline.

The game's story takes place six years after Link defeated Ganon in *A Link to the Past*. While the kingdom is at peace, Princess Zelda has a recurring dream of a shadow over a temple. When a mysterious light appears in the east of Hyrule, both Zelda and Sahasrahla's younger brother, Aginah, go to investigate.

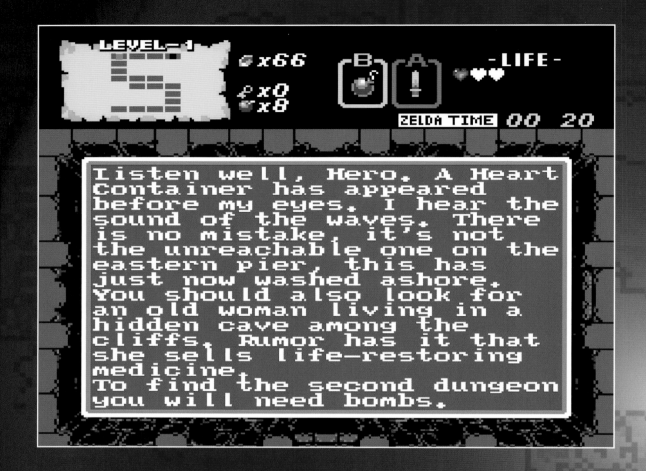

They find a young child lying on the ground and take the youth to Sahasrahla's hideout near the Eastern Palace, where Aginah now resides. Because of the young hero's clothing, they believe that the child may not be from Hyrule at all. Zelda learns that Sahasrahla has left the land to seek out Link, who departed after defeating Ganon years before. Sensing courage within the child, Zelda believes that they could be the Hero of Light.

We won't go too in depth with the game's plot for those that wish to play the game for themselves. The hero sets forth on a quest to retrieve ancient stone tablets in order to learn more on the impending evil. At the start of the game, the player has no weapon. Instead, prior to obtaining a sword and shield from the Eastern Palace, a golden bee in a bottle can be used to protect the player. When let loose, the bee will attack any monsters the hero encounters, but will run from those who wield a blade. Also given to the player is a bug-catching net and an ocarina which can be used to return to the entrance of a dungeon.

The game is set up over a timeline of four real-world weeks. Each week, an hour-long broadcast would be made, similar to that of a serialised story. The player would have a total of around fifty minutes to complete two dungeons, as well as explore Hyrule in search of secrets and bonuses. After the time limit is over, the player's progress would be saved regardless of their position in the game. Progress would be carried over to the next session, and players would keep any obtained tablets, items and rupees. Rather than allow players

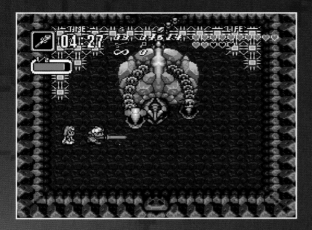 

to complete unfinished dungeons from the previous week, a thief stands at the entrance of the dungeon and would supply the hero with any treasures they had found within the dungeon.

The narrator from *BS Zelda* makes a return in the game, but Aginah and Princess Zelda also speak to the player through telepathy. Their dialogue comes in the form of voice acting and informs the player as well as advances the game's plot. The game also has timed events, which can change the weather to rain or fog and introduce Zora enemies, as well as give players temporary powers. Some timed story events can also occur, such as the player having to save Zelda from Octoroks or helping the Loyal Sage from drowning in a lake. The game was only ever broadcast twice and it was impossible to boot the title outside of the designated broadcast time, resulting in it being impossible to play without emulation. Because the narration was broadcast to the player live and not stored locally, it's impossible to emulate the game's voice acting and orchestral soundtrack without the original audio.

While not considered part of the *Zelda* canon, *Ancient Stone Tablets* is the first time in which Zelda is shown to predict future events through her dreams. It also marks

the first time Zelda's voice was heard. The game's plot takes place six years after the events of *A Link to the Past*, the same period of time between the release of both games in Japan. *Ancient Stone Tablets* was the first time non-playable characters would move around the world and change behaviour depending on the game's time, a feature used extensively in *Majora's Mask*. The term 'Hero of Light' would also be featured in *Four Swords Adventures* and is given to whoever is deemed most helpful during the multiplayer mode of Hyrulean Adventure.

The *BS Zelda* titles are both impossible to play without the use of emulation. ROM files of the games can be found on the *BS Zelda* homepage which was created in 1999 and is still maintained by Con. The site archives all releases of the games, as well as all patches available for the titles. These patches range from changing sprites to be Link during gameplay, to attempting to recreate the full original broadcast quality of the titles. Of course, these games never saw a release in America, but they were also only available for a very limited time in

Japan. In 1999, Nintendo broke its partnership with broadcaster St.GIGA, who controlled the service. And due to a dispute with the radio station, the service was officially terminated in 2000.

## Localisation

The Satellaview, or some variant of it, may have been considered for the international market at some point. Regional variations of the Super Nintendo all had expansion ports used by the Satellaview on their underside, making it possible to utilise a similar device. However, there were no equivalent services to St.GIGA that operated outside of Japan. This would have made it difficult to get a similar service working in the West. Audio or radio dramas were extremely popular in Japan at the time of the game's release, before the relatively recent explosion in popularity outside of the region, meaning the streams were tailored for a Japanese audience. In fact, many games had audio drama adaptations. Along with the cultural differences, the need to find voice actors for English release would have been costly, making the investment of localising the games an even bigger risk.

T:          DJ SLOPE
OLE:        SEGA DREAMCAST,
            SONY PLAYSTATION 2
:           2007
LOPER:      VIVARIUM INC.
ISHER:      SEGA
ON:         JAPAN

hh *Seaman*, the 'advanced Tamagotchi'
e where you have to look after and talk
ugly half-human half-fish hybrid who
antly mocks you and your lifestyle
es!

mes like this never normally leave Japan
e most part but this one did... well, in
rica at least with the narrator being none
than Spock, aka Leonard Nimoy! Sadly
Brits we had no choice but to import
boot it up via a Utopia boot disc as it
ieved that SEGA Europe wanted to get
ocumentary legend David Attenborough
ved but unfortunately wasn't able to.
wever, *Seaman*, as obscure as the
, is not the main focus of my section
*gion Locked*! Nope. Ya see, several
els and remakes of sorts came out after,
100% Japanese exclusive.
Japan, *Seaman* was quite a big hit. It
reated by Yoot Saito, who came up with
lea for the game as a child after visiting
seum and learning about coelacanth, a
es of fish once believed to be extinct.
ito-san himself was already popular
g gamers in Japan after releasing the
national hit *SimTower*, and as you may

have guessed he was pretty upset that his
*Seaman* game (as popular as it was) was
released on a system that was very quickly
becoming extinct itself.

Regardless, quite a few Japanese-
exclusive bits 'n' bobs came out during this
time to help ride the *Seaman* hype train,
including music and drama CDs, plushies,
toys, limited edition Dreamcast consoles, a
rerelease with improved audio recognition
and extra lines of dialogue, the Christmas
*Seaman* Dreamcast game which lets you

you are errrr 'lucky enough' to own a copy of the American release, put it
your CD player and listen to Seaman explain how you shouldn't be doing that
you may get a 'viral disease'… I'm not joking!

send messages to other Dreamcast owners, mobile phone games and my personal favourite: 'CONNECT! SeaMail', a desktop widget of sorts where *Seaman* would swim across your desktop screen, alerting you of emails and reminding you of appointments.

As bizarre as all of this was, it was far from the last we heard from our creepy (almost Marshall Mathers) looking fish-faced frenemy, as the first Japanese-exclusive PlayStation 2 game in the series came in the form of a remake of sorts, simply titled *Seaman*.

ASCII were the guys who helped port the software and two exclusive controllers were available for purchase alongside it. As the game is completely reliant on not only understanding Japanese but also speaking Japanese clearly enough for the microphone to understand you, they are completely unplayable for Western audiences. With that said, the GOLDEN circular 'Sea-Mic' is something I proudly own in my collection and is as hideous as it is gorgeous.

This version actually has a lot more under the hood compared to the Dreamcast original. Not only does it have improved graphics and audio recognition but certain features like the egg-hatching sequence in the fish tank has been removed and instead you find yourself in the ocean luring in Seaman with small bug larvae.

The feeding phase has also changed. Instead of having a small basket of grubs you now need to rip bark from a tree and get your larvae from there instead (with creepy faces included, of course).

Much of the rest of the game plays out the same, as you raise your Seaman back in the tank at the lab, talking to him and most of the time getting insulted. That is until it's time to return your Seaman back into the ocean where you will need to find a Sea-Woman to get them to mate... Quite the disturbing image I must say!

This is where the original Dreamcast game finishes. However, the PlayStation 2 version continues on land as a sort of Seaman-Frog being where you find yourself speaking with the Dreamcast's evolved Seaman-Frog standing next to a Dreamcast flag... Yep, a Dreamcast logo in a PlayStation 2 game... what a crazy world we live in!

Anyway, the PlayStation 2 Seaman-Frog and the Dreamcast Seaman-Frog then mate and give birth to an iguana-looking Seaman which you will need to teach to swim before letting back into the ocean, and if you succeed then congratulations, you just completed *Seaman* for the PlayStation 2.

A 'completed version' (aka a slightly improved version) came out shortly after and added a few bug fixes and hints to help players as well as reintroducing the egg-hatching sequence from the Dreamcast original. If you're a fan of the original and can speak Japanese, then this is the ultimate version of the game!

Still here? Trying to piece together what you just read? Crazy isn't it. As stated

Japan loved the world of Seaman, and to end my nightmare-fuelled segment there is just one more game in the series worth speaking about: *Seaman 2: The Peking Man Rearing Kit*.

Yep, Japan got an exclusive sequel to this obscure pet simulator, again for the PlayStation 2, and it's even more bizarre than what came before it.

The game starts off with you creating an entire island, similar to games like *Black & White*. Instead of looking after a fish in this game you look after a Peking man on the island and help him throughout his daily life.

As this game is more of a god simulator than a pet simulator you can control the weather to help your Peking man, which is done by using a battery indicator so that you don't overuse it. This can also be used to stun animals to help with hunting or start fires to help with cooking.

You click around the screen and interact with your Peking man as best you can. Limited at first, but as time goes on,

he learns to understand you and his environment more and more. You can tickle him to raise his happiness meter as well as feed him to reduce his hunger.

You can collect items found by the Peking man throughout the game as well as exchange them for other, more useful items, some of which are very much sponsored by third-party companies such as Japanese-branded chocolate or cans of Pepsi.

The original Seaman, which if you remember correctly changed from a sort of fish to a frog to a lizard, thankfully makes a return in this game and is now a Seaman-Bird. (Ya can't make this up.) Seaman-Bird claims to rule the island and is here to give advice to you from time to time in his witty fashion. Occasionally he even gives you items to help your Peking man along the way. He also doubles as the person you will need to trade collectables with, he sells you certain items, and best of all, he can tell

LIGHT

you your fortune. That is if you pay him to do so.

As the game goes on you will eventually find a Peking woman, which you will attempt to have your Peking man mate with, and if you do, as you would expect, a child is born. This is where the game changes from a sort of god simulation into a more appropriate sequel to the original. As the parents eventually die you are left to look after their son, who through using the advancements made in the first half of the game should evolve a lot quicker and eventually will gain a mobile phone so that he can directly communicate with you the player. *Seaman 2* is a rather obscure, yet brilliant sequel to the equally obscure and brilliant game with a funny name... hehehehe it sounds like something rude!

# SEGAGAGA

| | |
|---|---|
| **CONSOLE:** | SEGA DREAMCAST |
| **YEAR:** | 2001 |
| **DEVELOPER:** | SEGA |
| **PUBLISHER:** | SEGA |
| **REGION:** | JAPAN |

Anyone familiar with SEGA will tell you that the company's history is a rocky one. It was among the biggest hardware developers to come out of Japan in the nineties, but when consoles turned to disc-based technology their sales began to falter. SEGA's final attempt at a home console was the SEGA Dreamcast, a system that still has a cult following to this day. One of the last games developed by SEGA for the device was a love letter to fans filled with the characters and charm SEGA were known for. They called it *SEGASEGA*.

Released in March 2001, *Segagaga* is a bizarre RPG that referenced not only the company itself, but also a large number of SEGA's games and characters. The name is a play on the term 'being gaga' for something, and in particular, being gaga for SEGA. It was chosen in place of the name *Sega Sega*, as they hoped that reducing the focus on the SEGA name would be less intrusive.

Often abbreviated to *SGGG*, the title was directed by Tez Okano, who would later

go on to create *Gunstar Super Heroes* and *Astro Boy: Omega Factor*. Although the game is primarily an RPG, it covers a mix of genres. It defines itself as a 'SEGA simulator', with the game's plot and story loosely based on the reality of what happened to SEGA. In the game's story, SEGA is struggling financially against its leading competitor, DOGMA. SEGA's world marketplace share is a mere 3%, and without any signs of improvement. To fix this, the company plans to get kids from the street and introduce them to the company

**Dazz:**
*Segagaga* is absolutely nuts. I cannot believe that after over a decade of following fan translation news on this game, almost nothing has come to fruition. I've even taken a look at the data myself to see if I could help get this title playable in English... If SEGA is somehow reading this, please, for the love of all that is SEGA, rerelease this game. I will do all of its marketing; you can even pay me less than Okano, and I will commit to it with supreme dedication.

in hopes that their management can bring the company back to its former glory. The player takes on the role of one of those kids, Tarō Sega.

During the initial part of the game, the player is tasked with battling employees from various development studios within the company. This stage of the game talks about how the giant doors of the building are there to keep employees in, rather than keeping everybody else out. The high stress levels of developing games has caused them to become 'subhuman', something that the game proclaims is the 'unfortunate truth of the games industry'. Nobody has entered the development room in twenty years, and so none of the company's higher-ups really knows what is happening at SEGA. Sometimes they receive a finished product in exchange for food and water, but eventually somebody needs to go in and crack the whip.

This initial part of the game plays out like a standard RPG, with each studio being a maze filled with a variety of enemies. Some playful enemy designs are thrown into the mix, ranging from literal cut-out photographs of real developers within SEGA, bizarre creatures, and various mecha-forms of Ralph Macchio, the actor who played Daniel LaRusso in *The Karate Kid*. Unlike typical RPGs, battles don't unfold by exchanging physical attacks. Instead, the fight is an exchange of verbal abuse by commanding your enemy and insulting them. Telling them that they will never have a girlfriend or that their product

can't make any money, you will eventually weaken their will and defeat them.

With only a single party member and enemy in battle at a time, this is a fairly simple process. There are a number of special attacks that can be used, however, with interesting and unique results. Failing to defeat an opponent doesn't result in a game over, but instead removes a month of development time for the company, something that is extremely detrimental for the latter part of the game. After taking down an enemy, it's possible they'll want to join you on your quest and will try to negotiate for a job. This is performed through a ten-second segment of exchanging questions in quick succession, including what sort of salary they can expect to receive.

After the process of hiring, the game moves into its advertised simulation segment. Each studio brought in is made up of seven members: three programmers, three designers, and a director. These employees make up the total stats for a studio, providing them with Stamina, Creativity, Skill, and Speed. These all define how well a game is being produced, such as its quality, how quickly it is being

made, and how much budget is left. This leaves the player with a number of decisions, such as whether they want to create a skilled team to produce a few high-quality products, or just push out fast shovelware in a hope that it'll increase profits.[*] Other decisions can also be made, such as whether to overwork staff and reduce their stamina, forcing them into a vacation to recover, or letting them work at their own comfortable pace. There are a total of four studios that can be taken on board in total.

During this stage, random events can occur that change how well the company is performing. Staff can have both positive and negative events happen to them, which will either elate them or make them depressed, and affect relationships within the team. Specific orders can dictate how games are created, such as deciding to either rush development or delay a game to improve its quality when it reaches an alpha or beta build. After three years with the company, the game ends, and different endings can be achieved depending on how well you performed. The only way of failing the game entirely is by running out of funds before the three years are over.

[*]    Shovelware is low-quality and low-budget. They are simple games often mimicking existing products.

さてと。次回のお告げの儀は、明日くらいかな？

Dialogue between characters shows the real-life dilemmas that face game developers. The hero wants to create innovative and fresh titles that will attract new customers and help the company thrive, but many will say how such things are hard to achieve and the company's financial security is more important. The game's most well received element is its homage to SEGA's past. With constant cameo appearances, retro music, references to other SEGA games, and even bizarre minigames that throwback to previous SEGA titles, there is a huge amount of fan service for SEGA veterans. While we doubt many of you will ever get the chance to play *Segagaga*, we're giving you a warning that this next part details the game's ending.

**SPOILER ALERT!** In the game's climax, the player straps himself into an R720 unit, a parody of the SEGA R360 arcade unit, which results in him being shot into space. With the evil DOGMA corporation performing a hostile takeover, a huge cast of SEGA characters are sent out to battle them. This includes characters like Sonic the Hedgehog, Tails, Ristar, a variety of *Phantasy Star* characters, and the Bad Brothers from the first stage of *Golden Axe*. The player is pitted against a barrage of enemies in a shoot 'em up style game. The boss of this stage is a continually upgrading piece of SEGA hardware, which after each form is destroyed, will morph into the next console generation. This segment is similar to *Thunder Force*, particularly with the inclusion of an additional vessel reminiscent of the ship's design in *Thunder Force V*. *Segagaga*'s director, Tez Okano, would later go on to work on the *Thunder Force* sequel, *Thunder Force VI*, which launched on PlayStation 2. This game was originally in development for the SEGA Dreamcast, however, and some of the original assets are used in this final scene.

Though the Dreamcast launched with some success in Japan in 1998, their competition was fierce. The impact of the Dreamcast hitting the market was short-lived, and soon after its launch, sales figures began to tank. As a result of some internal arguments, the company decided that the console market was not a secure financial option for the company, and that they should instead dedicate their efforts into becoming a leading third-party developer, which allowed them to work without console restrictions. A result of this internal arguing was a lot of staff shuffling, and people both internally and externally thinking that the company was headed to its own demise.

When Okano initially pitched the title to SEGA's management, many believed his proposal to be a joke. After a second round of fund-seeking for the project, it was approved by Hisao Oguchi, the president of the now defunct SEGA development team Hitmaker. Okano estimated the total budget for the game came to 'less than a hundredth' of *Shenmue*, which is known for being a huge financial burden on SEGA with a budget of over $70 million. One factor that helped with the game's reduced production costs came from Toei Animation, who gave a discount to the developers on all animated footage.

*Segagaga* was released at a time when the Dreamcast's future was bleak. SEGA's schedule for upcoming high-quality releases was looking sparse, and they needed to do something that would bring in revenue. Just

two months before the game was released, SEGA announced the discontinuation of the Dreamcast. At this stage, *Segagaga* had been in development for two years in secret. Okano was concerned that after development was revealed 'anything could happen'. This is an important point, as one of the reasons the game was published was because SEGA was struggling financially, and they felt that the company wouldn't be portrayed in a negative light within the game. This way the company could portray their struggle with a comedic touch, getting ahead of bad press and pointing fun at themselves.

When *Segagaga* was initially conceived, there were around 300 copyright issues that needed to be resolved within the company. This was later brought down to just 100, meaning some of the game's ideas had to be scrapped or changed. These include the idea of having SEGA's famous SEGA Saturn mascot in the game, Segata Sanshiro, as well as a Ferrari. The franchises that ended up appearing in the game came as a result of their popularity with fans, as well as the availability from a legal perspective.

After the game launched, Okano stated that he was given a marketing budget of around $200. With such a small budget, he felt that one of the only methods of marketing a title as bizarre as this would be with a similar marketing strategy. Okano spent over half of the budget on a wrestling mask in order to hide his identity during signing events that he set up at four different locations across Akihabara. With support from the head of SEGA's PR, Tadashi Takezaki and Taku Sasahara from SEGA AM3, the game was able to obtain a full-page newspaper article, which helped to increase awareness and popularity for the title.

これまでにない企画で、
新しいゲームを作り

The game launched with respectable sales through SEGA's online store, ultimately leading to a full retail release. With its popularity, a budget version of the game was also released some time later.

## Localisation

Despite reasonable sales, it's not surprising that the game was never localised, as the target audience was extremely limited even within Japan. The Dreamcast which had already been discontinued at the time of the game's launch, and SEGA's lack of financial stability, are likely contributing factors to the lack of translation. The game also makes heavy use of text and has a huge volume of characters and cultural elements that don't translate well for a Western market. Reworking all these elements into a narrative that makes sense to Westerners would be time-consuming and expensive. Not only this, but the previously mentioned licensing issues would need to be renegotiated all over again for different markets. Efforts were once made by a group of fans to translate the game, but with no news coming out in almost seven years at the time of this book's publication, it's unknown if the game will ever be playable in English.

# SUIKODEN II'S JAPANESE CARD GAME & VISUAL NOVELS

The *Suikoden* universe is one that Konami had made several attempts to expand upon, though with limited success, particularly outside of Japan. While the core series was translated and released in the US, three different games were created based around the highly revered second entry into the *Suikoden* series. *Suikogaiden Volumes 1 & 2*, and *Suikoden Card Stories*.

## GENSŌ SUIKOGAIDEN: SWORDSMAN OF HARMONIA

CONSOLE:      SONY PLAYSTATION
YEAR:         2000
DEVELOPER:    KONAMI
PUBLISHER:    KONAMI
REGION:       JAPAN

## GENSŌ SUIKOGAIDEN: DUEL AT CRYSTAL VALLEY

CONSOLE:      SONY PLAYSTATION
YEAR:         2001
DEVELOPER:    KONAMI
PUBLISHER:    KONAMI
REGION:       JAPAN

*Gensō Suikogaiden: Swordsman of Harmonia* was released in August 2000 for the original PlayStation. The title sees the player take on the role of Nash, a member of the Holy Harmonia's Southern Border Defence Force. The first volume of the two-part visual novels is set during the same period as the Dunan Unification War featured within *Suikoden II*. The game was translated by a dedicated team of fans led by Rin-Uzuki and is now completely playable in English.

   As a visual novel, the game's mechanics are simple. The player's interactions with the game are mostly to progress through the game's text, but there are several choices thrust upon the player. These choices result in branching paths to the game's story, giving the player some control of the events that play out. The player is provided with points at varying intervals of the story, which can be used to make certain choices at select moments of the game. If the player doesn't have enough points, they will be forced to follow a particular option.

Nash's mission is to infiltrate the Jowston City-States and investigate the rumours that one of the twenty-seven true runes has surfaced within the area. The story begins in the midst of his adventure as he is escorting Sierra Mikain to Muse in the hopes that she will be a good lead. Nash is accompanied by a number of characters found within the *Suikoden* universe, and in many cases provides them with more background and alternate angles on the events that occur within the second game of the series.

With the game often dipping into earlier events, it reveals that Nash actually makes an appearance within *Suikoden II*, though in disguise as a soldier who allowed Jowy and Riou to enter a supply tent within an army camp.

With Volume 1 marking Nash's first appearance within the *Suikoden* universe, Volume 2 would further expand upon his story, while also helping to breach the gap between the second and third mainline *Suikoden* games.

*Gensō Suikogaiden: Duel at Crystal Valley* was released a year after its predecessor and follows Nash's journey home to Harmonia. The story takes place three months after the unification of Dunan, with Nash looking to get revenge against Zaj Quilous, a man who has torn Nash's family apart.

This story leads him to meet more characters of the *Suikoden* universe and helps introduce plot elements and locations that would go on to appear in *Suikoden III* a year later.

Nash's journey sees him travelling through the Grasslands of *Suikoden III*, where he encounters a village celebrating the legend of the Flame Champion who brought a stop to the invasion of Harmonian soldiers on the land sixty years prior.

Due to the popularity of Nash's character with fans, he too would go on to appear within the mainline sequel which is set fifteen years after the first volume of *Suikogaiden*. This would be his first appearance to a Western audience.

# GENSŌ SUIKODEN CARD STORIES

**CONSOLE:** NINTENDO GAME BOY ADVANCE
**YEAR:** 2001
**DEVELOPER:** KONAMI
**PUBLISHER:** KONAMI
**REGION:** JAPAN

In 2001, Konami published a Game Boy Advance adaptation of the physical *Suikoden* collectable card game. Developed by software team Will, the release surprised many with the shift from Sony's PlayStation to Nintendo's Game Boy Advance. *Gensō Suikoden Card Stories* is a retelling of the story of *Suikoden II* with the only major change being that battles are now played out through a card game, though a number of plot elements and the sequence of events have also been adjusted. Unlike *Suikoden II*, however, the emphasis is shifted from the game's story to the battles.

The game begins during the ambush against the Unicorn Youth Brigade as the player is attempting to escape the camp. If you've never played *Suikoden II* then we would recommend doing so in order to understand the title's story instead of using *Card Stories* as a means of learning it.

Battles play out like this: players draw a hand of cards. The goal of a battle is to obtain a set number of victory points. By clearing missions on the board, VP can be earned. Cards are used to attack with various stats, but also to set up missions on the board to be completed. The number of VP earned for clearing missions is determined by each card, often rewarding the player placing the card fewer times than their opponent should they win the skirmish. Once a mission is put into play, the opponent has their chance to attack it first.

Missions involve placing a leader character, followed by other units. The same character cannot be played twice, regardless of how many cards for that character you have in your hand. Each mission has a number for how many points need to be obtained to clear it, with points being earned by adding additional units to the fight.

After a mission has been cleared, one character must be left behind to claim the card. With each turn between missions, the player's hand will be refilled, and the battle continues until somebody obtains all VP necessary. There is more to the game with various stats coming into play.

The game was translated by Pokeytax in 2013, with the bulk of the game now available in English. At the same time, this patch will also make a card that was previously unavailable appear within the game. Pokeytax notes that this card meant that in the Japanese release, it was impossible to complete the game. It would have been made available at special events and through promotions, but due to *Card Stories'* poor sales, this plan never materialised. The patch also restored an inaccessible cutscene.

## Localisation

Sadly for the West, two of the least popular Japanese genres when it comes

172

to localisation in America are card games and visual novels. The *Suikogaiden* games were developed by a separate team to that of *Suikoden III*, and after completion of Volume 2 of *Suikogaiden*, both teams merged, working together on subsequent *Suikoden* releases.

*Suikoden Card Stories* had very little impact on the Japanese market, and with a failed physical card game release to go alongside it, it was highly unlikely that the game was ever considered for international release. You probably shouldn't expect to ever see official releases of anything *Suikoden* ever again unless it's a pachinko machine.

# SUPER BACK TO THE FUTURE PART II

**CONSOLE:** NINTENDO SUPER FAMICOM
**YEAR:** 1993
**DEVELOPER:** DAFT
**PUBLISHER:** TOSHIBA
**REGION:** JAPAN

The *Back to the Future* series has an infamous background with video games. Many pieces have been written about the notoriously slated NES adaptation of the film franchise. Even Bob Gale, co-creator of *Back to the Future*, showed disdain to LJN's North American NES creation.

Most early *Back to the Future* tie-in games are seen as generally poor and lacklustre in the West, with very bland and unimaginative ways of using the interesting and expansive concepts shown within the movies. That's why it's curious that Japan received an adaptation of the American series that took the ideas in a different direction.

Released in 1993 by Toshiba, *Super Back to the Future Part II* was developed by a software house called Daft. Clear Japanese roots are shown in the game's art style, opting to use a more Japanese style of artwork referred to as 'super deformed', or 'SD' for short.

Following the story of the film, Marty has returned from his adventure in the first *Back to the Future* film. While visiting his girlfriend, Jennifer, Marty is approached by Doc Brown, who has just returned from a trip to the future. He informs the pair that their kids are in danger, and so they travel to 2015 to stop Biff's grandson, Griff, from causing trouble. However, trouble kicks up again when an elderly Biff takes an old sports almanac back to 1955 with Doc Brown's DeLorean, giving the book to his younger self. When Jennifer, Marty and Doc Brown return to 1985, they find their home has been plagued with crime, Doc Brown has been deemed insane, and Biff is now Marty's stepfather. Marty must travel through Hill Valley and figure out why this has happened, and how he may solve it.

DOC: Marty, you've got to come
  back with me!
MARTY: Where?
DOC: Back to the future!

The player takes control of Marty McFly, who navigates stages using his hoverboard. The player is unable to get off of the hoverboard, making the game much faster by nature; an element that proves difficult with the game being quite limited in its field of view. The hoverboard also allows Marty to take out foes by jumping on their heads.

Marty can jump, perform a spin attack, or gain additional speed. Stages can be tricky to navigate, with many branching paths, but boss fights are generally considered to be somewhat less difficult. Some stages hide away bonuses in locations that can only be found through blindly jumping offscreen; however, the game also hides death traps in the same way.

Coins can be found in each level which, when enough have been accumulated, can be spent on vending machines to purchase power-ups, health restoratives or additional lives.

Whilst visually appealing to some, *Super Back to the Future Part II* has its fair share of flaws, most of which were not uncommon for this period of gaming. Many consider the game's level designs to be unfairly difficult and that the controls take some time to master. There are also complaints of slowdown in some areas.

## Localisation

The game was clearly created with a Japanese audience in mind, opting for colourful anime-style graphics above the more traditional Western approach. It's possible that the game was made with this limited audience in mind, and no plans for the game to be localised outside of Japan. As we've seen many times, licensing franchises for game adaptations can be a major limiting factor in the legal process of publishing a game overseas. Not a huge volume of information is available on this game's development process, having been made by a team that has now disbanded and only ever seen Western exposure through their budget titles.

While entirely playable without being in the player's native language, a fan translation of the game was created by mteam, which translates all of the game's dialogue and stage title cards to English.

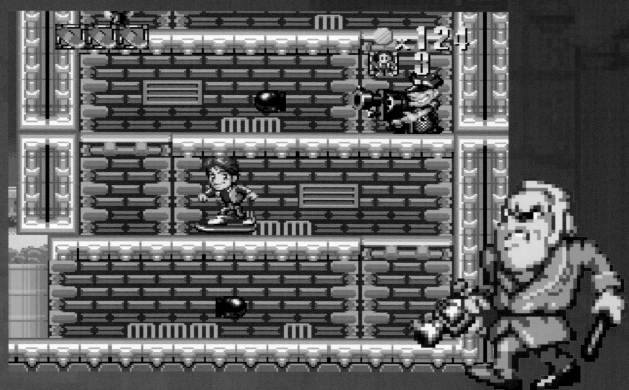

# SUPER GALDELIC HOUR

**CONSOLE:** SONY PLAYSTATION 2
**YEAR:** 2001
**DEVELOPER:** EXRAYS
**PUBLISHER:** ENIX
**REGION:** JAPAN

We've previously mentioned Enix in this book. In their history of releases, a slew of titles were released that would be hit or miss with a lot of the gaming audience. Their attempts to capitalise on their strongest ability, developing RPGs, made the company look like a one-trick pony. So, when a developer approached the publisher showing off a game that was like nothing they had seen before, it's possible that their reaction was to use this title as a way of broadening their market. Little did they know that this was one of the last times the company would be credited as Enix alone, as soon after the company merged with Squaresoft to form Square Enix.

Super Galdelic Hour is an extremely bizarre game released in 2001 and developed by Exrays, a company who had only worked on two other titles prior to *Galdelic Hour*'s conception, which were also Japan exclusives.

The title is unsurprisingly pushed toward an older male audience, with the game concentrating heavily on the characters' busts and backsides. The game's camera angle and 3D models are brought up negatively in many reviews, stating that they give the game a creepy 'uncanny valley' feel. Uncanny valley is an issue with computer-generated or robotic humanoids in which

**Greg:**
It's difficult to know what to say about this besides the obvious – saying the game is weird is an understatement. I can imagine a teenage version of myself absolutely loving this (FOR NO SPECIFIC REASON) but playing it now, it just makes me feel a little uncomfortable. The game in itself is an average party game at best but unless you're a pubescent teen the novelty wears off very quickly. At the very least it's an interesting cultural piece but no prizes for guesses as to why it was never brought westward.

attempts to form more realistic visuals can come across as creepy or unnatural.

The game's story follows stuffed animals that are transformed into busty women after a radio wave was discovered and used on them. These are Toko the rabbit, Neko the cat, Kuma the bear and Coco the fox. These characters are known as 'QTS', a play on the English word for 'cuties'. From a spacecraft being used as a broadcasting station, a scientist created his own guerrilla television channel called QTS Jack TV. The game takes place as a fictional game show played on this station.

The game's manual poses a number of interesting questions about this plot without actually answering many of them. These include what the game's name actually means, as well as the size of the

characters. With that said, it does tell us that the characters defecate by excreting a pachinko-sized ball that smells of raspberries.

The show is made up of various competitive skits which are played in the form of different minigames. Typically these games are built around erotic themes, or simply used for titillation.

The games include:

**Hip Sumo Wrestling**: Two characters compete to knock their opponent off a floating platform into a pool of water by thrusting their backsides against one another.

**Quick Draw a Pie:** A game similar to Simon Says. The player must hit the action button when the word 'go' appears on screen. The quickest player wins.

**Skipping Rope:** A simple jump rope game in which the player presses a button to jump. Well-timed jumps provide the bonus of weird camera angles.

**Go! Go! Rolling!:** Rotate the left analogue stick in a clockwise or anticlockwise direction to reach the top and bottom of the screen.

**Eccentric Puncher:** A boxing game in which the girls wear large inflatable boxing gloves and must beat each other up. This minigame is notably perceived as a very negative element of the game, as the girls are shown visibly beaten after the game finishes.

Only a few games are available from the game's start, while others can be unlocked by progressing through the single player mode. By performing well, you'll be rewarded with money to be spent on customisation items for the various characters. With each run through of the single player mode, more sponsors will also be obtained which will increment the volume of money earned with each completion.

## Localisation

While *Super Galdelic Hour* is a very peculiar game, it was received pretty well overall in Japan. Many people cited that it was a great way of trying to branch the PlayStation 2 console out into new directions, allowing for creativity with bizarre results to be enjoyed.

However, the game's lack of localisation shouldn't be too hard to understand. The PlayStation 2 at the time of this game's release was only two years old, and it's highly likely that Enix considered the game to be of more interest to the Japanese market. The sexual themes and odd story would have likely been a point of contention in the US. Many companies felt that the PlayStation audience was better known for its purchasing of titles with more serious tones. To top that off, minigame compilations were often considered to be only passable. In an article about what was being played in Japan at the time, the game was brought up on IGN with much disdain, demonstrating the typical Western mentality regarding these sorts of releases. Please note that we aren't stating this as a positive or negative response.

The game had very little following online after its release, and in Japan is still considered to be a relatively forgettable title. This is with the exception of one cosplayer, Omi Gibson, who went all out with her outfit depicting the game's lead character, Toko, in 2011.

# SWEET HOME

**CONSOLE:** NINTENDO FAMICOM
**YEAR:** 1989
**DEVELOPER:** CAPCOM
**PUBLISHER:** CAPCOM
**REGION:** JAPAN

The survival horror genre was made popular in the West with Capcom's release of *Resident Evil*. The first entry in the *Resident Evil* series was produced by Tokuro Fujiwara, a developer who had been working in the industry for some time when he was given the opportunity to create the initial title in a series which would go on to be one of Capcom's most recognised franchises. He took a bulk of his inspiration from a NES title that he had previously worked on, using many mechanics that are considered to be core elements to the survival horror genre. That game is called *Sweet Home*.

Released in 1989, *Sweet Home* was based on a Japanese horror film of the same name, also released in 1989. Tokuro Fujiwara took on the role of the game's producer but was supervised by the director of the original movie, Kiyoshi Kurosawa.

The game's story is the same as that of the original film release, following a film crew as they explore the abandoned

---

**Matt Barnes:**

I checked out the *Sweet Home* film. The film wasn't bad; genre-wise it went all over the place. I was interested to see if *Resident Evil* took anything from the original film that its predecessor was based on. Though these might be a bit tenuous, I did find a couple of things. The story of the film reminds me heavily of the demo of *Resident Evil 7: Biohazard* – a small camera team heading to a haunted mansion in order to film a documentary. The opening of *Resident Evil 7* had a similar setting, with a long forest road leading up to a big locked gate of the mansion. It also has a heavy emphasis on an ancient key to access the main door, and the style of shot in which the key is revealed feels very 'Resident Evil'. Otherwise it didn't really have much more that gave me any Resi vibes.

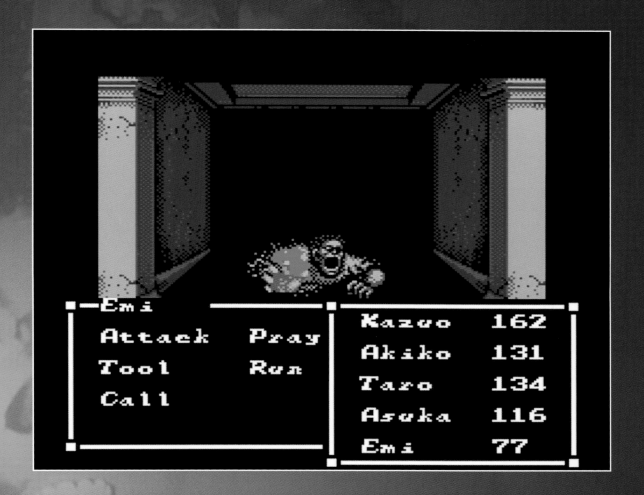

| Emi | | |
|-----|---|---|
| Attack | Pray | |
| Tool | Run | |
| Call | | |

| Kazuo | 162 |
|-------|-----|
| Akiko | 131 |
| Taro | 134 |
| Asuka | 116 |
| Emi | 77 |

home of the presumed-dead painter Ichirō Mamiya. He was known to have hidden several paintings within the mansion before he mysteriously disappeared thirty years ago. The documentary team of five are attempting to seek out and recover these lost frescos from the crumbling mansion, but upon entering are trapped inside by a ghost who threatens to kill them for trespassing.

Now left with no other options, the crew must split up and work out a means of escape, all the while facing dangers from monsters found throughout the building, as well as the unstable nature of its structure.

They discover the ghost's identity to be Lady Mamiya, the late wife of painter Ichirō. It is revealed that thirty years ago, their two-year-old child had fallen into the house's incinerator and was burnt alive. In order to provide her dead son with playmates, she kills several other children so that they may be with him in the afterlife. A short while later she committed suicide, and with her ghost unable to be at peace, she became trapped within the mansion.

Movement and battles play out similarly to most turn-based RPGs, with some changes to the mechanics to give the game a more survival-horror feel. During fights, the team is able to attack to deal physical damage with their equipped weapon. They can also pray to power up attacks, and call to teammates to switch control over to them, allowing them to make their way to the fight and lend assistance. Items can also be utilised for various effects, and each unit is able to run. Each party member is considered an individual, and thus running during fights requires all members to escape. The option of running is dangerous, as it can result in the abandonment of a crew member, leaving them to deal with an enemy solo.

Each of the five characters has a role within the group. Cameraman Taguchi is capable of revealing hidden images, art restoration expert Asuka can use her vacuum to clear broken glass, the kind-hearted Akiko is able to heal her companions, Kazuo can make use of his lighter to burn away obstacles, while his daughter Emi is the master of unlocking.

By talking with teammates, you are able to form groups which will assist in progressing through the mansion quickly, as well as dealing with enemies in battles with greater ease. Travelling alone is an incredibly dangerous option and will likely result in death.

By using their tools throughout the mansion as a team, they must solve puzzles, defeat monsters and attempt to get out alive. They're assisted by items spread throughout the mansion, which can be picked up and swapped amongst the party. These items don't just include objects that will assist in progress past puzzles and obstacles, but also weapons and armour which can improve character stats.

These items can be swapped with other items anywhere in the mansion and remain there until being picked up again later. This is an important element to solving puzzles, as limited inventory space and how the player manages it comes into play. In order to solve some puzzles, the team must backtrack, assisted through the mansion's array of alternate doors that can be unlocked.

Quick time events can occur too, requiring the player to make snap decisions under the stress of permadeath. Party members may be killed at any moment as the result of traps and dangerous obstacles, with no means of revival. The unique skills of each character can still be utilised however, as items that pertain to their talents can be found near their corpses. Depending on the outcome of the team and which members of the crew survive, it's possible to see one of five different endings.

*Sweet Home* was one of the first home console games that Tokuro Fujiwara had worked on. When speaking with Kiyoshi Kurosawa about the creation of an adaptation of his movie, he was told 'not to worry if the game doesn't follow the movie exactly'. Fujiwara stated that he was able to use the film as a reference, and that with both the movie and studio set at his disposal, he was able to use whatever elements he felt would work within the game. He stated that he was considerate of how to go about adapting the film into a game, adding extra elements to the story through diary entries from fifty years prior to the events of the game.

*Sweet Home*'s successor, *Resident Evil*, was originally conceived as a remake of this 8-bit title. Fujiwara initially invited Shinji Mikami onto the team, *Resident Evil*'s director, with this goal in mind. He believed that Mikami had a good grasp of understanding what is frightening, later recounting, 'Mikami hated it. This is how our conversation went: "You hate being scared?" "Yep." So I figured we should do it. If he'd answered that he never got scared, I couldn't have trusted him with the project. People who aren't afraid of anything don't

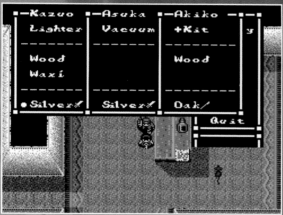

understand what's frightening. In my view, you can't make a horror game if you don't have any fear.'

Fujiwara was frustrated with his work on *Sweet Home*, mainly in terms of graphical fidelity. When talking about *Resident Evil*'s roots, he stated, 'Once the PlayStation was released, conversation turned towards the idea of launching an original franchise. The basic premise was that I'd be able to do the things that I wasn't able to include in *Sweet Home*. It was mainly on the graphics front that my frustration had been building up. I was also confident that horror games could become a genre in themselves.'

## Localisation

The game's region-locked status is often cited online as being due to the high levels of gruesome imagery and strong adult themes, with Nintendo wanting to keep the family-friendly appearance of the NES. However, no official source states this. It's quite likely that another reason for the game being kept within Japan was due to the nature of its adaptation status.

While the game is incredibly fresh and innovative for the time, it was still an adaptation of a film that also saw no international release — even today it would be considered obscure, if not for the game's legacy. It's unlikely that an international release was ever considered.

# TALES OF DESTINY 2

**CONSOLE:** SONY PLAYSTATION 2
**YEAR:** 2002
**DEVELOPER:** WOLFTEAM, TELENET JAPAN
**PUBLISHER:** NAMCO, SONY
**REGION:** JAPAN, TAIWAN, KOREA

With the *Tales* series having already received several Western releases, it's interesting to see which games were never brought overseas. While there are several games within the series that never received English translations, one of note is a direct sequel to a game that was localised in America: *Tales of Destiny 2*.

The history of *Tales of Destiny 2* is of particular interest. In the US, a game published as *Tales of Destiny 2* was released in 2001 for the PlayStation. This game is actually more known to fans and original Japanese players as *Tales of Eternia*; however, when it was decided it would be brought overseas, the game's creators stated that the change of name was made to help the game's sales through brand recognition. *Tales of Destiny* was the first of the series to be localised in the West, and so to improve sales, the team decided to change the name in order to show a clear connection between the two releases. Of course, this caused some confusion later down the line when a true sequel to *Tales of Destiny* was created and published in Japan under the same name of *Tales of Destiny 2*.

This real sequel, released only a year later in 2002 for the PlayStation 2, put players back into the same fictional universe featured in the first title. The game's plot follows a world that has been damaged by the impact of a comet a thousand years prior to the game's events. In an attempt to generate heat and energy during a

prolonged winter brought on by the comet's arrival, the people of this world used a gemstone that had been brought with the comet known as Lens. With this power, a floating city known as Dycroft was created, which would be the beginning of a conflict between the people of the city and those who lived beneath it.

A group of scientists who had defected from Dycroft developed living weapons known as Swordians for the people of the Earth, giving them an advantage during this conflict. Eighteen years prior to the events of the first *Tales of Destiny* game, this war begins to re-emerge, and during the events of the title, the Swordians find new masters. In the first game of the series, the player takes on the role of the wielders of these

weapons who work to bring peace to the world, but in doing so damage the planet. The sequel begins eighteen years after this occurs.

Stahn and Rutee, two of the heroes who wielded Swordians, have had a son named Kyle Dunamis. Kyle lives at an orphanage run by Rutee, though with the establishment looking to run out of funds, Kyle betrays his mother and goes to find money to keep his homestead running, and in doing so discovers a type of gemstone, a giant Lens. He meets a girl named Reala who emerges from this stone, who claims that she is in search of a hero. Kyle wishes to fulfil the role of a hero and keep his parents' legacy alive, and so follows Reala to prove himself as being capable. After finding the Lens missing, officials arrest Kyle and his friend Lori who accompanied him on his journey, only for them to escape with the assistance of a mysterious swordsman known as Judas. Kyle soon finds himself fighting against the

assassination attempts brought on by a man name Barbatos Goetia, who is attempting to wipe out the fighters who had previously worked to bring peace to the world. Kyle learns the true identity of the assassin who murdered his father when he was just five years old: Barbatos.

If you've ever played a game within the *Tales* series before, you'll likely have a strong idea of how the game's mechanics work. Characters explore the world like any other RPG, but with battles occurring on a two-dimensional playing field. This battle system is a trademark of the series known as the Linear Motion Battle System, featuring real-time combat. The player takes control of characters one at a time, with the remaining units being controlled by a customisable AI. Commands can be issued to the team through a battle menu, allowing the player to have control over the team's combined actions.

Characters have several skills at their disposal for dispatching enemies, such

as basic attacks, stronger attacks known as Artes, and exceptionally high-damage attacks called Mystic Artes.

The game's combat system allows for multiple players to participate, giving the option for a four-player co-operative experience as opposed to just a single player; while common in the *Tales* series, it's a rarity among long-form story-based RPGs. It's also possible to allow the game's AI to take control of all characters at once.

Outside of battles, a number of optional side-quests can be taken on, and a cooking mechanic is included to allow the player to create several dishes which will provide bonuses during combat.

Development of the game began after work had ended on *Tales of Eternia*, taking roughly two years to complete. It was developed under the working title of *Tales of X* and was created after the team behind *Eternia* was considering its next step. A direct sequel to *Destiny* was decided after they considered the large volume of lore for the first game, and how the world could be expanded by following the next generation of characters within it.

The game's developers hoped to be able to show Kyle's journey into becoming a hero, and producer Makoto Yoshizumi likened the plot elements of learning from a wise

teacher to that of *Star Wars* or *Indiana Jones and the Raiders of the Lost Ark*. To provide the game's atmosphere, work was made to balance fantasy elements with those of reality. The team's desire was to create, as they stated, the 'ultimate 2D RPG', as they saw many PlayStation 2 RPG releases at the time work with 3D.

*Tales of Destiny 2* was announced in February of 2002 and released later that same year. Localisation of the game occurred in China and South Korea through the efforts of Sony a year later, and Sony wanted to include the game in part of its world tour promoting the next generation of console RPGs. However, issues arose with this plan due to rising tension between America and Iraq. Their official response to cancelling this world tour was as follows:

'It is reported that the situation in the United States and Iraq is becoming tense in recent press reports. We carefully watched the conditions of the situation towards the tour, but there are still no signs of the situation resolving between the two countries, and the dangers of terrorist activity in various parts of the world cannot be denied. We have decided that it is difficult to conduct the tour under these circumstances, considering the safety of everyone as top priority. To the tour winners and accompanying guests, we apologise from the bottom of our hearts for this decision. Thank you for your understanding.'

## Localisation

During a launch event for the game, producer Makoto Yoshizumi was asked if an overseas version was being developed, to which he stated that he was uncertain. No news was released to suggest a translation was worked on, but with the game looking to make an appearance in America, it's likely that plans had been considered at one time. The game was later ported to the PlayStation Portable in 2007, once again only being released in regions that the game had initially been published within.

While efforts had been made by a team known as Phantasian Productions to publish a fan-translation patch for the game, the only

available translation is a pre-alpha release which provides an incomplete early translation of the game's menus. The last news to come regarding the game's translation directly was in 2008, but the team's coordinator, Cless, posted in 2016 that he has had personal issues that have kept him away from his efforts to work on translations.

**CONSOLE:** SUPER FAMICOM, SUPER NINTENDO ENTERTAINMENT SYSTEM
**YEAR:** 1995
**DEVELOPER:** QUINTET
**PUBLISHER:** NINTENDO, ENIX
**REGION:** JAPAN, EUROPE/AUSTRALIA

Quintet are a company renowned for their RPGs published on the Super Nintendo, such as *ActRaiser*, *Soul Blazer* and *Illusion of Gaia*. The president of Quintet was Tomoyoshi Miyazaki, who was also the scenario writer of the first three games in the *Ys* series. The company's main director, Masaya Hashimoto, was the programmer for those same *Ys* titles. Their games were known for addressing darker themes, in particular the balance between life and death. These titles all had two worlds that were not only the opposite of one another, but complementary, needing to exist for either to operate on its own. One game that follows these ideas most closely is the Japan and PAL exclusive game *Terranigma*.

Quintet's *Terranigma* was published in Japan in 1995 and was released in the European and Australian markets fourteen months later. The game follows the

same gameplay style as the previous games in what many call the 'Soul Blazer Trilogy'. The game is played from a top-down perspective and attacks are performed in real time. These moves change depending on whether the hero is running or jumping while attacking, and the player is also capable of blocking projectile attacks with the shoulder buttons; however, the player is not capable of defending against melee damage.

Throughout the game, the player obtains new equipment such as armour and weapons, as well as items that can be used to improve the player's stats. As with most RPGs, experience is gained by defeating enemies, eventually resulting in a level up which improves the player's stats. The game also uses a shop system with money dropped by enemies.

Rather than the standard use of magic attacks with an MP meter, the game opts to use magical rings that can be purchased from stores. These rings can be bought with not just the money obtained from enemies, but also collected Magirocks. These are rocks found throughout the game and serve only as a tradable item. The rings are depleted after

use but will give the player their Magirocks back so they can repurchase the rings. Additional rings also become available as the game progresses.

The story of *Terranigma* takes place on a fictional version of Earth; however, unlike our planet, this Earth is hollow and features two distinct landscapes. On the surface or 'Lightside', intelligent new life is born, resulting in rapid progress and development. In the underworld, or 'Darkside', there is little besides fear and anger. These two sides came to be known as 'God' and 'Devil'. After billions of years of conflict between the two factions, a last stand took place on the continent of Antarctica revealing no true victor. After the great battle, the continents of the Lightside sank beneath the ocean and the entrance to the Darkside was sealed.

The story follows Ark, a young man who grew up in the lone village of the underworld, Crysta. Ark's brash nature leads to him opening a forbidden door. Within, he discovers a mysterious box from which a

demon named Yomi emerges. Their meeting causes time to stand still within the village, leaving the citizens frozen in place. The only person left unaffected is the village's Elder, who guides Ark to lift the curse that has befallen the other villagers.

Ark then leaves his home, a first for the people of Crysta, and must conquer a trial set across five towers, each representing a different continent of the planet. After he succeeds and life is brought back to the village, he is instructed by the village Elder to travel to the Lightside and restore it to its former self. Ark sets off on his journey, leaving all that he knows behind.

The reason for the game's localisation, and lack thereof, comes from the way in which Enix operated its business at the time of the game's publication. As the game was published by Enix in all territories, it would have been up to them to publish the game in the American market, too. However, around the time of *Terranigma*'s release, Enix made the business decision to close its American

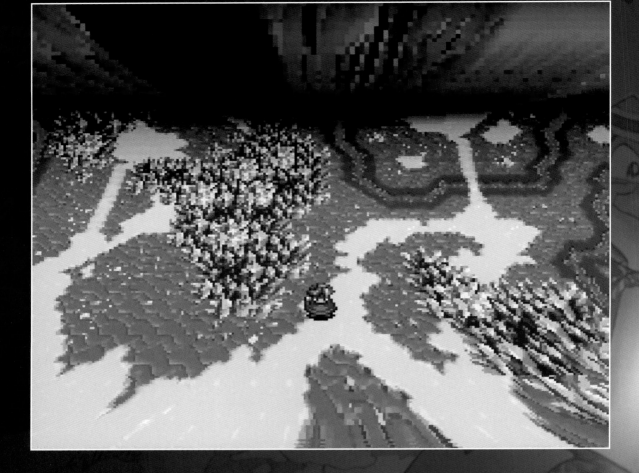

branch of the company and halt all future game releases in the region. Enix made this decision due to the poor sales figures of their games in the region.

Meanwhile, the game was given a full official English release in Europe and Australia after Nintendo opted to localise and publish the game in those areas. Beyond this, the game was also given official translations in German, French and Spanish. The translation team even featured Daniel Owsen, a translator for Nintendo of America who had worked on many AAA first-party titles. Owsen was also one of the first voices heard on a Nintendo console, providing his voice not only for *Star Fox*, but for the introduction to *Super Metroid* as well.

## Localisation

In some ways, people consider the game's lack of official US release to be positive. American releases of SNES titles from the previous two games in the *Soul Blazer* trilogy were known to have instances of censorship, while *Terranigma* remained the same in all of its releases. While it's a shame that the US audience weren't able to play the game at the time of its release, it does mean that if the game is ever published through digital distribution in the future, it's possible that the game will feature the uncensored European release.

We're tiny but
we're happy we are
useful to someone.

| CONSOLE: | SONY PLAYSTATION |
| --- | --- |
| YEAR: | 1997 |
| DEVELOPER: | DREAMFACTORY |
| PUBLISHER: | SQUARE |
| REGION: | JAPAN |

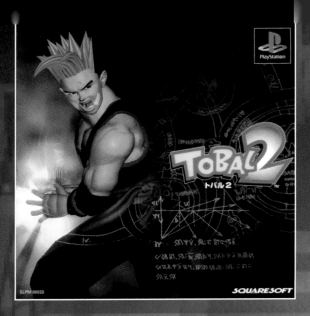

Squaresoft are known for their RPGs, but sometimes they like to mix it up. This was evidenced by their well-documented PlayStation 1 fighting game *Ehrgeiz: God Bless The Ring*. With a host of original characters and characters from their 1997 RPG *Final Fantasy VII*, the game saw a positive response from fans of the company. Squaresoft had another game developed with DreamFactory, like *Ehrgeiz*, called *Tobal No. 1*. This was released to the world, but not its sequel, *Tobal 2*, which saw vast improvements over the first title. Before we talk about the second title, we'll talk a little bit about *Tobal No. 1*.

Tobal No. 1, released in 1996 by DreamFactory and Squaresoft, had everything going for it. The team behind the game included veteran fighting-game creator Seiichi Ishii, the director and designer of not only *Tekken* but also *Tekken 2*.

The story of *Tobal* takes place on a planet simply called Tobal, a world with large quantities of Molmoran, a type of ore used for its energy source. In the year 2027, the planet's ninety-eighth tournament is being held to decide who has the right to use the ore.

The title features a total of eight characters with four additional fighters that can be unlocked. Each character has their own plot, but the game's ending is the same for each. The characters are Chuji Wu, Gren Kutz, Fei Pusu, Hom, Ill Goga, Mary Ivonskaya, Epon and Oliems. Most of

**Greg:**
The main reason we haven't made a video on this is because the game is insanely difficult, and we couldn't gather the footage. What was that?! We're not terrible at video games, YOU'RE THE TERRIBLE ONE. Having played the first game a lot as kids, we went into this game with all the best intentions and high hopes for another fun fighter/beat 'em up combo. Unfortunately, the only thing that took a beating was our egos as the tutorial dungeon repeatedly slapped our sacks until we just called it quits. If you give it a go, good luck and Godspeed.

the unlockable characters are bosses from the game. These are Mufu, Emperor Udan, Snork and Tori-Bot. Snork isn't technically a boss and is instead a smaller version of the large boss, Nork. Tori-Bot, or Toriyama Robo, is named after the game's artist, Akira Toriyama. Toriyama's previous works include the famous *Dragon Ball* series and the Squaresoft RPG *Chrono Trigger*.

The most interesting aspect of *Tobal* is in its quest mode. While the game is a standard fighting game, also included is a dungeon crawler that makes use of the title's fighting mechanics. The player must advance through the dungeon using elevators, avoiding traps and participating in fights with a collection of monsters and the other playable characters. Also found in the dungeon are a variety of stores for buying and selling items, a pivotal aspect to

progressing in the dungeon. Items perform a variety of different actions, such as healing, unlocking doors, or improving your character's stats. At the end of the dungeon is a boss battle, which after completing will unlock that character for the main game.

The controls for this portion of the game are remarkably poor. While attempting to convert the fighting controls to a 3D environment with the need for jumping and movement in 360 degrees of direction, an element of control is lost. The difficulty of this mode is steep.

The game's soundtrack was created by a total of eight composers who worked for Squaresoft. These include the renowned Yoko Shimomura, composer of the *Kingdom Hearts* soundtracks, and Yasunori Mitsuda, composer of the *Chrono Trigger* series.

*Tobal No. 1* sold over 660,000 copies in Japan, making it a successful release.

In America, however, the game only sold 20,000. In total, America only made up just under 13% of the game's total sales, while Japan took 72% of all sales in the world.

With such a high volume of sales, DreamFactory and Square saw fit to create a sequel, entitled *Tobal 2*.

*Tobal 2*, released only a year later, sees a vast volume of improvements over the first title in the series. The graphical fidelity is improved greatly, with characters displaying more emotion when shown closely. The fluidity of the combat is also vastly better than its predecessor, with the game able to be played at sixty frames per second.

The most praised aspect of *Tobal 2* compared to *Tobal No .1* comes in its quest mode. While the first game simply throws the player into a generic dungeon, *Tobal 2* attempts to tie the world together with a story, NPCs, a village, and proper adventuring. The controls of this mode are still fairly poor, but it was well received for its attempts at expanding the fighting genre. The player is also capable of earning experience points for each part of the character's body, allowing them to improve the damage done by each type of attack, such as punching, grabbing or kicking.

However, *Tobal 2* is most notable for its roster of fighters. While the characters from the original are still there, two new fighters were introduced. These are Chaco, a female fighter dispatched by Galaxy Patrol to the planet of Tobal in order to explore an evil 'ki' emanating from the planet, and Doctor V, a surgeon from a family of military background, exploring ancient techniques to take medical science to the next level.

However, *Tobal 2* currently holds the gaming

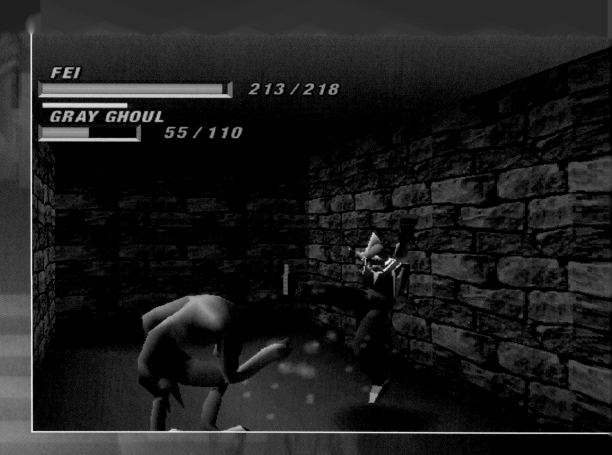

FEI 213 / 218

GRAY GHOUL 55 / 110

world record of featuring the largest character roster of any fighting game, with a total of 200 to choose from. This large number is made up of the monsters featured throughout the game's quest segment, which can be captured and unlocked for the game's versus mode. While a vast number of these monsters are just recolours or reskins of the same enemy, featuring the same moves, there are some unique monsters to be found. This includes a cameo from *Final Fantasy*'s Chocobo creatures which can be used to battle.

## Localisation

*Tobal 2* saw around 350,000 sales, still significantly more than the first game sold in America. An official at Square stated that it was originally intended for the game to receive a Western release, but it was subsequently cancelled. Sales for the first

game were poor, and so releasing a sequel would have made no sense. Most people only bought the game's original release because of a *Final Fantasy VII* demo that was included in the case. It was rumoured that some third-party companies had an interest in publishing the game in the West, but Square didn't want to provide the licence to another company. It was also stated in an issue of the official PlayStation magazine that the game wasn't translated due to the PlayStation 1's limited memory, making the English dialogue too long to fit within the title's text boxes. Luckily, a fan translation exists created by Infinite Lupine. The patch translates the game's quest mode, making it fully playable. It was even released before the official PlayStation statement was made, making this official reason seem rather dubious to say the least.

# TWIN CALIBER

**CONSOLE:** SONY PLAYSTATION 2
**YEAR:** 2002
**DEVELOPER:** RAGE SOFTWARE
**PUBLISHER:** RAGE SOFTWARE
**REGION:** EUROPE

When it comes to gunplay action, many in the games industry will look to movies. Something we often see games attempting to replicate is the pure action of dual wielding some guns. While many games do have options for dual wielding pistols, it's often never truly replicated with the same sort of action capable within film and television. This is due to aim typically being dedicated to a single reticle on screen, meaning that you're effectively firing two guns into the same location, and not in different directions at different targets. One on-rails co-op shooter title that attempted to change this was *Twin Caliber*.

    *Twin Caliber* was released exclusively in Europe in 2002 for the PlayStation 2 by Rage Software, a now bankrupt British team from the city of Liverpool. The game features two-player co-operative gameplay,

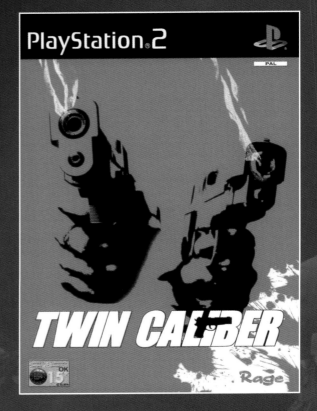

although a single-player option is available which will provide the player with an AI controller partner. The title plays like most

**Matt Barnes:**
I honestly still do not know if this is a good game or not. It has a ridiculous plot, a terrible script and the controls are just plain stupid. The camera is a real problem too – it feels like it's on rails whilst simultaneously shifting slightly in the wrong direction when aiming. But I have to admit that once you get the hang of it, it can be incredibly fun, especially two player. The way each character swings their arms around shooting every bad guy with absolute precision without moving their heads makes me feel like I'm in the lobby scene at the end of *The Matrix*. I'm pretty certain this whole game was based on that scene, just without the jumping kicks and the lobby, and I'm honestly fine with that.

arcade-era on-rails shooters and features a total of twenty-six stages. It attempted to combine the world of games and movies, featuring cinematic camera positions with gameplay built entirely around the mechanic of operating two guns at the same time.

With the player walking through stages autonomously, it gives the player the ability to concentrate on making use of both of the character's weapons. The game lets the player dual wield through both analogue sticks, with both sticks controlling the player's respective arms with full 360 degrees of rotation. A gun's line of sight is pointed out for the weapons to help make aiming slightly less asinine, an issue that comes from the game's camera often shifting around to suit the game's predetermined path and scenarios.

Due to the need for multitasking, the game requires a lot of practice for the player to be able to concentrate and consistently hit their mark in two different locations. Although this mechanic is the unique aspect to the work, it can also be disabled to map both weapons to the right stick alone.

Special weapon ammo is limited, though through the use of checkpoints can be restocked, where the player's health can also be refilled. While friendly fire is also considered to be the true way in which the game should be played, it too can be disabled.

Boss fights often require the player to shoot at two areas simultaneously, causing issues for players opting to have both guns tied to the same control mechanism. It also causes a requirement of learning to adapt

to this new form of gameplay. The manner in which boss fights must be executed is often left fairly ambiguous, or in some cases hidden through misleading cues.

The game's plot follows John T Fortman, a sheriff caught up in the middle of a zombie apocalypse. After a mysterious young woman turned up in the small town of Sweet Liberty, rumours began to spread of a sinister cult developing. It took a month before all hell broke loose and people began to mutate.

With his fellow officers of the law out of commission, Fortman finds a partner in an unlikely yet clichéd turn of events. With nobody to assist in taking out the creatures, he turns to another survivor within the prison's high-security wing, Valdez, an inmate on death row. The two

fight their way through the town, killing hundreds as they go.

## Localisation

The game's lack of localisation in America comes from the developer's lack of experience in publishing games, though not in the way that is usually the case with most region-locked titles. Rage Software filed for bankruptcy a year after *Twin Caliber*'s launch within PAL territories, after the company sought to expand its reach beyond just a development studio and become a publisher too.

The team had little success as it took on this new venture, with many of the titles released being slated in reviews and selling well below expectations. The largest of disappointments for the team likely came when one game tanked despite their expensive brand deal with the professional soccer player David Beckham.

With *Twin Caliber* being one of their final releases before closure, it's of course not surprising to hear that efforts to take the title overseas would have been fruitless. At the time of its closure, Rage Software was considered to be one of the oldest game development studios within the UK, with offices spread across six cities. If the team did manage to take *Twin Caliber* to the United.States, it would have likely been of little salvation, as the title was also panned by critics and saw only a limited run within the company's home country.

# VALKYRIA CHRONICLES III

**CONSOLE:** SONY PLAYSTATION PORTABLE
**YEAR:** 2011
**DEVELOPER:** SEGA, MEDIA.VISION
**PUBLISHER:** SEGA
**REGION:** JAPAN

SEGA's popular *Valkyria* series has resonated with a Western audience. This might have something to with its first title establishing a war-torn world not too different from our own. With added fantasy elements and a unique combat system, it was well received on the PlayStation 3 in 2008. In 2010, a direct sequel was released worldwide for the PSP, which was followed by a third game in 2011, also on the PSP. However, this third title never saw release outside of Japan.

*Valkyria Chronicles III* kept many of the mechanics of its predecessors, but also made several adjustments to improve the accessibility for newcomers. The *Valkyria* games feature a combination of both real-time and tactical roleplay elements that come together to form the BLiTZ system (Battle of Live Tactical Zones). The player is assigned missions and must then plan out a team of units for the assignment. During battles, the player can select a unit they wish to move from an overview

of the map. Moving units will deplete the action gauge, limiting the distance they can

**Dazz:**
I loved the first *Valkyria Chronicles*, but the second never sat well with me. It lacked a lot of features and polish I would have expected of a sequel — moving to a portable console, they ended up missing. The third game, while limited, fixed these issues with their own new features; something that actually worked quite well. The game's story was a great look at alternative events surrounding the first game, and to be honest, I was pleasantly surprised considering the game was released as a portable title.

travel. To complete the unit's movement, a single action can then be performed. While a unit can be selected and given a command multiple times, this will limit the other units for the player's turn. Using a unit multiple times will provide the player with a smaller amount of action gauge with each consecutive selection.

The game has five types of unit: Scouts, Shocktroopers, Engineers, Lancers and Armored Soldiers, with each having tactical benefits over the others. After each mission, the player is able to bolster their squad by spending their money and experience points. A total of nine units can be dispatched on a mission, with many characters having their own unique skills known as 'potentials'. These potentials define the character as a unique soldier within each fight and can provide both positive and negative effects in battle. However, a unit's battle potentials are skills that can be learned and honed throughout the game, allowing them to grow as a

soldier. Some characters also have special abilities that only they are able to perform.

The game's plot takes place during the Second European War, paralleling the events of Welkin's squad in the first game of the series. The player follows Kurt Irving, Imca and Riela Marcellis, who are assigned to Squad 422, known by many as 'The Nameless'. They're what's known as a penal military unit, comprised of deserters of foreign armies and criminals whose names have been struck from records and have no identification besides a number. The unit is ordered by the Gallian military, often tasked to perform the most dangerous missions that are refused by the militia and the army.

With the motto '*Altaha Abilia*', meaning 'Always Ready', the team are forever willing to accept a mission against all odds.

The team is made up of Soldier 7, Kurt Irving, who was previously an army officer and hopes to redeem himself after being falsely accused of treason. Soldier 1, Imca, who's a Darcsen heavy weapons specialist looking for revenge against the Valkyria that destroyed her home. And there's Soldier 13, Riela Marcellis, a young woman unknowingly of Valkyria descent. The squad's major task is to combat against an imperial unit shrouded in mystery known as the Calamity Raven, primarily consisting of Darcsen soldiers. Many of the higher-ups within the Gallian Army will send the team on missions that could reflect poorly on Gallia if the mission goes wrong. This is because the squad is off the records, and the higher-ups have plausible deniability if the squad is discovered or commits any collateral damage. This has many effects during the war, leading to successful incursions, but also some dire consequences for the people within the unit. Many consider the third entry in the *Valkyria* series to follow a much darker tone. The trilogy's musical

composer, Hitoshi Sakimoto, stated that several of his original compositions for the game's theme were rejected. He had to rework the theme roughly seven times, and even adjusted individual pieces of it with a synthesiser before bringing it all together again. He wanted the battle theme to give players a sense of a 'modern battle' and remove any fantasy elements from the scenario by including modern instruments. The instruments would work together to create atonality, meaning a lack of functional harmony or central tone. This description and style is thematically similar to The Nameless unit, being made up of many different chaotic members that are hard to define.

The team began work on the third iteration in the series as soon as development had concluded on the second. They felt that they could refine mechanics that had been developed in *Valkyria Chronicles II* now that they had experience with the PSP. During a Q&A session, producer Shinji Motoyama stated that he doesn't have any preference when it comes to platform, but

understands fan desire for a new entry on a home console. But, he concluded, 'When selecting a platform, we have to make careful considerations, and with this, the reality was that we couldn't easily advance on the PS3. However, I want to say one thing: as developers we absolutely did not want to make a PS3 version that simply reused the materials and engine from [*Valkyria*] 1.'

Takeshi Ozawa, the game's director, also stated that the development staff consider the third entry to be 'the first sequel in the series'. This is due to the difficulties found when transitioning to the PSP hardware from the PS. The team had to work through a lot of trial and error before finding a comfortable working environment, which they felt affected the quality of the second game. With the third game on the PSP, the team could use the knowledge they had gained to improve on areas that felt substandard.

## Localisation

SEGA's manager of console sales, Hiroshi Seno, confirmed at the end of 2011 that the third *Valkyria* game would not be receiving an international release. The reason behind this was the unpopularity of the PSP platform in North America and Europe. To be able to undertake a translation effort, the second entry in the series would need to have sold enough copies to justify the costs involved, which it did not. However, an unofficial fan translation began development only a few months after this statement was made. After two years of production, the translation patch was completed and now allows users to play through the Extra Edition version of the game in English with ease.

# VIB-RIPPLE

**CONSOLE:** SONY PLAYSTATION 2
**YEAR:** 2004
**DEVELOPER:** NANAON-SHA
**PUBLISHER:** SONY INTERACTIVE
ENTERTAINMENT
**REGION:** JAPAN, EUROPE

The PlayStation brand has always had an element of experimentation at its foundation. With popular games that rely on a player's rhythm, the *PaRappa the Rapper* series is a highlight of the PlayStation consoles for many. The team behind the series, NanaOn-Sha, made frequent attempts to push gaming in new directions, as was evidenced with their original PlayStation game *Vib-Ribbon*.

Whilst *Vib-Ribbon* was exclusively released in Japan and Europe, it later saw a digital release in the USA. However, a Japanese-exclusive sequel to *Vib-Ribbon* which changed its experimental direction was *Vib-Ripple*.

Released in 2004, *Vib-Ripple* took *Vib-Ribbon*'s concept of including your own music in games and changed it to inject photos into games instead.

The player is put in control of Vibri, a vector-based rabbit featured in the game's predecessor. Each stage is made up of a photograph in the form of a trampoline on which Vibri must bounce. Through well-timed button presses that match up with the game's music, Vibri jumps, each jump varying in height. Jumping in the correct areas of the photo will release items called 'Peta Characters'. Before the time runs out, Vibri must collect all of these Peta Characters in order to win. These characters range from dogs to trees to ice-cream cones.

The location of Peta Characters is hinted at by the shape, colour and size of icons displayed at the side of the screen. By using these hints, the player has to try to work out the location of items. When drawing close, the controller vibrates and a drumming sound can be heard.

Vibri must also avoid enemies called 'Boonchies'. Bumping into a Boonchie will reduce Vibri from a rabbit to a frog, then to a worm, eventually killing her off entirely and resulting in a game over. By collecting Peta Characters, Vibri is able to evolve beyond her rabbit state, becoming Super Vibri, a form that is capable of physically hitting Boonchies which will freeze them in place. This form also allows the player to see hidden Peta Characters.

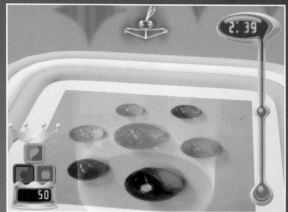

At the end of each stage, Vibri will present the player with new Peta Characters which are stored in an album to take a look at any time.

The game contains a total of sixty photographs provided by default. Through the use of the PlayStation 2's USB ports, it's possible for the player to add their own stages to the game via a digital camera or mobile phone, which will be scaled to just 200x200 pixels in resolution. Photos can also be added through the console's online service. It's possible to save these photos to a memory card, with twelve photos taking up roughly a single megabyte.

## Localisation

The game's lack of localisation likely comes from the game's experimental nature. Having created a number of titles which experimented with a variety of concepts for Sony in the past, it's possible that Sony didn't see wide commercial potential for the game.

# WONDER PROJECT J: MACHINE BOY PINO

**CONSOLE:** NINTENDO SUPER FAMICOM
**YEAR:** 1994
**DEVELOPER:** ALMANIC
**PUBLISHER:** ENIX
**REGION:** JAPAN

The life-simulation genre requires players to raise a character they don't directly control. In the nineties, the genre was popularised with digital pet toys like Tamagotchi and Digimon, but even before then, it had its place in the gaming world. Life simulations where the player raises a specific character were coined 'raising sims' and have been popular in Japan for some time. The long-running *Princess Maker* series is a good example of a raising sim, requiring the character to raise a daughter to become a princess. Enix took this raising sim concept and created a game built around a story of peace called *Wonder Project J: Machine Boy Pino*.

   Published by Enix in 1994 for the Super Famicom, the game was developed by *E.V.O.: Search for Eden* developers who left Technos and formed a studio called Almanic. Graphically, the art style can be compared to the works of Studio Ghibli or early Japanese anime. It pushes the Super Famicom to its limits, featuring a huge array of animations and actions that can be performed by the

mechanical boy. The game has you watch over this mechanical child, whose

**Dazz:**
I had only ever seen images of *Wonder Project J*, and that was enough to sell it to me. Visually, this game is stunning, but in terms of gameplay, it is absolutely brutal. Repetitive, but charming — something almost expected of this genre during these earlier days of gaming. The truth is, *Wonder Project J* is nothing but a collection of beautiful art and animation... but really, if that's all you're going in for, you won't be disappointed.

default name is Pino, accompanied by an interface robot named Tinker who looks like a fairy.

In the game's world, robots known as Gijin have lived among humans for the last fifty years. Contempt has been steadily increasing among the two groups, and the few human sympathisers of Gijin are often arrested. Our young boy's creator, Geppetto LaMark, is one of these human sympathisers. Dreaming of a perfect Gijin that can live as a human, LaMark created a young robot. He had only one task left: to fill all the boy's heart circuits. This would teach the boy what it is to be human and awaken the fabled J Circuit. Before Geppetto finishes his task, however, the government intervenes and takes him away, leaving the boy to fend for himself. The player is tasked to help raise the boy as a human and fulfil the old inventor's dream. As the young Gijin is almost indistinguishable from a real human, many of the people on the island mistake him for one of their own.

The player uses Tinker to instruct the boy how to use objects correctly, as well as helping him grow his abilities and understanding of the world. In many cases, he won't understand what's being instructed, and will attempt to eat live chickens whole or worship objects for no good reason. To combat his naturally boisterous actions, the player can praise him for using items correctly. If he

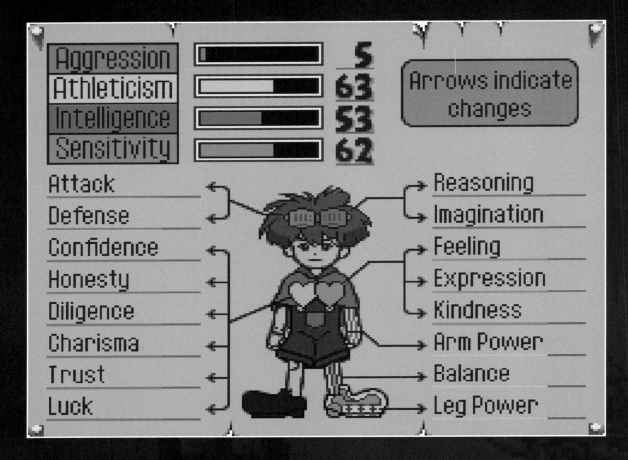

| Aggression | | 5 |
| Athleticism | | 63 |
| Intelligence | | 53 |
| Sensitivity | | 62 |

Arrows indicate changes

Attack → ← Reasoning
Defense → ← Imagination
Confidence → ← Feeling
Honesty → ← Expression
Diligence → ← Kindness
Charisma → ← Arm Power
Trust → ← Balance
Luck → ← Leg Power

acts in a manner the player doesn't like, they can scold him, teaching him to not do it again. By teaching with care and tough love, the player and Pino develop a bond.

Encounters throughout the island challenge the boy's understanding of the world by testing if he's capable of solving basic problems and performing tasks for other residents. These tasks encompass a number of skills and personality traits, including picking locks on chests, and even fighting. The player must adjust their mentality when dealing with each situation, having the child's kindness stats be high when dealing with animals, but less so when entering competitions. While the game's pacing is quite slow due to continuously training the child, there are a few segments with more action. The title has dungeons the player must help Pino navigate, instructing him to attack where needed or preventing him from walking into traps.

The player can purchase equipment from the item shop in town to assist with training, such as weapons and books of increasing difficulty. Items can also be fed to the boy to restore his health, grant him temporary buffs or completely alter his abilities.

The overall goal is to ease hostility between humans and Gijin by forming personal connections between yourself, the child, and the co-inhabitants of Corlo Island. With multiple endings, *Wonder*

The game's story is often compared to Pinocchio, given both tales are about a man named Geppetto, whose creation becomes a 'real boy' – one called Pino, the other Pinocchio. That said, an article in the UK magazine *Super Play* refers to Dr Geppetto as Dr Jebet Lamarq, the Geppetto name coming from the fan-translation team WakdHacks. The story is also likened to *Peter Pan*, due to the fairy-like Tinker.

*Project J* provides many options for how players can work to solve this problem.

## Localisation

The lack of localisation outside of Japan possibly comes from *Wonder Project J*'s themes, requiring the player to sometimes smack the boy to teach him wrong from right. Corporal punishment was falling out of fashion in the US at the time, partly due to research indicating it was more harmful to child development than previously thought. The game is also dialogue heavy and could be costly to translate. Any additional cost would reduce a game's chances at financial success.

Aside from these possibilities, we couldn't find sources for why *Wonder Project J* never came to the West. However, as the game received a sequel that also remained a Japanese exclusive, we can only assume the decision wasn't influenced by a lack of sales or interest.

# ACKNOWLEDGEMENTS

Thank you for getting to the end of our book — we had a great time putting this together, but none of it would have been possible if not for a handful of rather special people.

A massive thank you must go out to our YouTube community, who welcomed our videos with open arms. Thanks to you, not only have we managed to continue working on creating a resource for others to learn more about games they otherwise wouldn't have, but we've also had a fantastic time doing it.

Thanks to Shane from DidYouKnowGaming for giving *Region Locked* a chance on the channel, and to everybody who has supported us on our journey. Alex Daniels, our good friend and man-in-Japan who has helped on several occasions, translating bits and pieces.

The general gaming modding community, be they translators or not. With their contributions into the modding scene, it has allowed fan-translations to really thrive. Of course, on that note, we really must thank all of those involved in the fan-translation community — with their efforts, more and more people are gaining access to games that would otherwise be closed to them. The Aeon Genesis team in particular has been an incredibly inspiring group, as well as Clyde 'Tomato' Mandelin and his blog, *Legends of Localisation*.

Those who have made direct contributions to this book — DJ Slope, Guru Larry, Ashens, and Caddicarus for their guest articles. And who could forget everybody from Patreon, or who helped fund our book with Unbound — without whom, you would not be reading this very text on this very page.

Thanks to Shaun Tidnum, who created the custom sprites that appear throughout the book and on the cover.

# INDEX

Unbound is the world's first crowdfunding publisher, established in 2011.

We believe that wonderful things can happen when you clear a path for people who share a passion. That's why we've built a platform that brings together readers and authors to crowdfund books they believe in — and give fresh ideas that don't fit the traditional mould the chance they deserve.

This book is in your hands because readers made it possible. Everyone who pledged their support is listed below. Join them by visiting unbound.com and supporting a book today.

Pekka Aarnio
Jason 'Ultimacron' Abbott
Ed Abell
Yitzy Abramowitz
Alfonso Acosta
Andrew Acosta
Matthew Adcock
Mason Addis
Matt Addison
Tristen Adhikamangala
Andrew Adolf
Geechy Adrien
Aetherm
Vishal Aggroia
Agred
Samuel Ahboltin
Eric Ahn
Eric Ahnell
Omar Al Arti
Mohammed Al Owayyed
Ian Albanese
Olof 'Sarato' Albiin
Jose Roman Alcaraz
Heriberto 'Finn' Alejo
David Allan
Ashley Allen
Ben Allen
Hallie Allen
Stefan Alm

Abdulaziz Alnujaidi
David Altieri
Brandon Alvelo
James Amarant
Tim Amato
Lunar Amethyst
Nathaniel Ammons
Avi Amon
Albert Andeliz
Brady Anderson
Kyle Anderson
Nate Anderson
Parker Anderson
Cayden Andrews
Maria Angell
Angiru
AnotherMemory
George Apav
Craig Appleby
Hiroo Arai
S.A. Araquistain 'Vasconium'
Rosemary Arbogast
Michael Arnone
Luke Ashby
Tharglet Asimis
Ryan Atkin
Jordan Atkins
Nick Atkinson
Jonathan Attfield

Taygh Atwal
Olivia Stephanie Ault
Boghos Avedikian
AzzanRyu
Chance B
m b
Elias B.
Gavin Babb
Justin Bader
Gina A Baeza
Jake Baigent
Dakota 'DaxMax64' Bailey
William Bailey
Lewis Baines
Matt Baines
T. L. Bainter
Darren Balboa
Zackary Balderrama
Geoff Ball
Jeff Ballard
Zachary Balym
Francesco Bambace
Cliff Bambridge
Fabian Banks
Ryan Banks
Kyle Barch
Jeremy M Barker
Parker Barnard
Hunter Barndt

Michael Baron
Chris Barrett
Alexis Barroso
Carmen Bartkowska
Mike Bartos
Dalibor Bartoš
Andy Bashford
Elizabeth Basser
Marco Bastian
Daniel Bateman
Suzanne Baunsgard
David Michael Baxter
    (Es8802)
Robert Beard
Martin Becke
Nicolas Bédard
Ross Beedham
Peter Beerbaum
Chad Behr
Zachary Behrmann
Keir Beigel
Adrian Belcher
Glenn Beliën
    (LangeManGlenn)
Cory Bell
Josh Bell
Katie Bell
Eddie Beltran
Samuel Bennett
Shane Bennett
Joseph Benson
Laszlo Benyi
Manuel Berger
Michael Bergeron
Michael Bernier
Justin Berrios
David Bertie
Gregory Best
Victor Beucher
Kaedhen Bharathae-Lane
Julian Bieder
Benjamin Bien
Charlotte Birch
Athena Birck

Brian Bishop
Daniel Bishop
Davey Bishop
bjørn.spiegel
Ryan Blackburn
Dalton Blackwell
Phillip Blackwell
Kelly Blades
Max Blair
Victoria Blanchard
Brandon Blankenship
James Blanton
Jonas Blättermann
Tom Bleek
Dominic Boachi
Joshua Bock
Blair Bodnar
Michael Bohl
Gregory Bohnert
Axel Boidard
Christopher Bolling
Tom Bombadildo
Garrett Bonds
Jean-Baptiste Bongrand
Alexandre Bonin
Dennis Bönnekamp
Joel Bonomini
Eric Borck
Max Borushek
Justin Bourdon
Sven Bovens
Katrina Bowen
Tomaz Bowers
Parker Bowling
Alex Boyce
Danny Boyd
Bruno Branco e Brito
TJ Brandt
Sascha Brehl
Tom Breitenfeldt
Trond Kjetil Bremnes
Rory Brendan
Michael Brennock
Sheldon 'PenSolo' Brewster

Matthew Brigham
Mike Broadhurst
Alice Broadribb
Tom Broadwood
Logan Brock
Henry Brooks
Adam Brown
Dylan Brown
James Brown
Luke Brown
Michael Brown
Tyler Brown
Christopher Brownlee
Piia Brusi
Daniel Bryant
Tristan Bryant
Richard Bucci
Jacob Bucciarelli
Marvin Buckland
Kevin Bucknall
Chris Buldo
John Bull
John Bunday
Josh Burkey
Lazlo Burns
Matthew Byerwalter
Tyler Cady
Rob Callahan
Ross Cameron
Adam Cammack
Ethan Campbell
Ryan J. Campbell
Michael Card
Jared Cardozo
Alex Cardwell
Daniel Carlson
Antonio Carrero
Francisco Carretero
Alec Carter
Jeremy Carter
John Carter
Kevin Carter
Connor Casey
Scott Casey

Ian Cash
Filippo Casola
Raymond Cason
Jonnathan Castillo
Kristy Castillo
Miguel Castillo
Allan Paul Castro Coronel
Rick Cederholm
Sigh Cha
Marcus Champion
Tommy Chapman
Pavlos Chatzipantelidis
Robert Cherry
Jared Cherup
David 'TheBlablaman'
    Chhean
Rob Christopher
Jonathan Chu
Thomas Church
Dario Cirillo
Rhys Clarihew
Brennan Clark
John Clark
Tony Clark, Faye Young,
    Penelope Clark
Cooper Clay
Jake Clayton
Rayce Clemmer
Jillian Cleveland
Cat Clogston
Katheryn Clow
Geoffrey Cochran
Trey Cochran
Anthony Cocorikis
Daniel Codd
Cory Coles
Jonathon Coles
Regan Colley
Rob Collini
Jarom Lee Collins
Matthew Collins
Arthur Colombo
Caleb Colter
Hugh Condon

Ryan Conneely
Michael Consoli
Kathryn Convery
Nick Cooper
Adam Cooperman
Sean Cope
Emanuel Cordisco
Ethan Cornett
Bruno Correia
Joe Cortese
Dante Cosentino
Edgardo Cossu
Christopher Costigan
Ben Cottee
David-John Cousins
Melissa Cousins
Ryan Covell
Daniel Cowan
Cole Cox
Robert Cox
Angelique Crawford
Max Crawford
Andrew Crites
Mark Crosby
Kiel Cross
Blake Crossman
Eric Crowley
James Ryan Cruz Jr.
CrystalLakeManagment
Jason Culak
Philip Cullen
Charles Culley
Justin Cummings
Catherine Curl
Justin (Nick) Curtis
Takuya Curtis
Nicholas Czaplinski
Zachary Czarnecki
Piotr 'pecet' Czarny
Kelly A. D'Ambrosio
Adam Dalla Costa
Chad 'SaintCathedral'
    Danforth
Spencer Darbouze

John 'Darlo' Darlington
Mitchell Darroch
Nicholas Dastolfo
Sullivan Dausch
Juliet Davie
Alexander Davies
Christopher Davies
Colton Davis
Haley Davis
Joshua Davis
Parker Davis
Matt Dawidowicz
Adrian Dayrit
Ignazio De Guglielmi
Anthony de Jesus
Dik de Jong
Michael De Lellis
Joseph De Maria
Elizabeth 'Senmurv' Dedman
DeepfreezZ
Ignacio del Río 「V-Rator」
Guillaume Delafosse
Adam Demmon
Kyle Dennis
Wayne Denny
Monica DePaul
Carlos Deras
Jochem Derksen
Derphlosion
Fernando Deschapell
Jake Desmon
Sebastian Deußer
Dylan DeVore
Félix Dewaleyne
Akashdeep Dhaliwal
Austin Dherit
Michael Dichiera
Shaun Dickens
Darien Brice Dickinson
Andrew Dickman
Nathan DiDonato
Joseph DiOrio
Cristian Dispensa
Bryce Diuri

DJM (MASTERxBLASTER)
djtravz
Brasco Donnsen
Grant Donoghue
Carolyn Dooley
Tiago dos Santos Silva
    from Porto, Portugal
Joshua Doss
Pat Doswell
Eoin Dott
Tyler Douglas
Patrick Dovale
LMP Dragon
Duc Du
Pascal 'Pasu' du Bois
Alex Duff
Susan Duffy
Kevin Dugan
Pierre Gabriel Dumoulin
David Duncan
Stephen G Dunne
Shaun Dupont
Karthik Dwarki
Dan Dyer
Asher Dykstra
Lucas Eastwood
Lukas Ebner
Brandon Eckel
Michael Eckert
Nate Edison
Henrik Edlund
Kyle Edmond
Brenin Edmunds
Ben Edwards
Euan Edwards
Joenathan Edwards
Douglas Effler
Mary Effler-Li
Trym Eiken
Christoph Eisenberger
Thomas Ellinson
Jackson Elliott
Justin Lee Ellis
Michael Ellner

Alexander Emam
Robert Entemann
Robin Eltvik Erdal
Odd Einar Erland
Ottone Erminio
Alec Erreygers
Francisco Escudero
Mario N. Espinoza
David Espling
Juuso Etelämäki
Erik Evans
Neil Evans
Mark Evenson
Aarron Ewart
Roy Fadavi
Luke Faith
Marco Falciglia
David Falck
FallenAngelSamurai
Nombre Falso
Nico Fangmann
Gerry Sean Fearon
Joe Fell
Michael Ferguson
Jose Fernandes
Carl Ferro-Fields
Bonnie Fiddis
Chris Field
Angel Figueroa
Tomasz Finc
Scott Fine
Jordan Firari
Brian Fiscus
Joshua Fisher
Andrew Fisher
    @merman1974
Alex Fitez
Sarah Fitzgerald
James Fitzpatrick
Owen Flanders
Luke Fletcher
Scott Fletcher
Ludwig Flich
John Flickinger

Leo Flora
Federico Floris
Justin Flynn
Willy Foley, Joey Castaldo
Fabio Fonseca
Benjamin M Ford
Cole Ford
Grant Ford
Tom Ford
Felix Foreman-Mackenzie
Ross Forshaw
Jake Fortner
Joshua Foss
Alexander Föttinger
Ryan Fowler
Stuart Fowler
Noah Francis
Drew Frauts
Brent Frazier
Blake Freeman
Brandon French
Matthew Fridman
Rachel Friemel &
    Damon Jackson
The Friman
Fro-Zach
Louisa Frost @frostedLouie
Arielle G
Del Gagnier
David Gagnon
Andreas Gaisbauer
Miguel Galarza
Gil Galindo Bucio
Anthony Gallagher
Ben Galley
Seph Gallistel
Carl-Christian Gallon
Richard Paul Gamblin
Dickson Gan
Kenneth Oneal Gan
Erik Garcia
Lewis Garcia
Wilfrido Garcia
Clay Gardner

Zack Gardner
Kiersten Garfoot
Christopher Garland
Edward Gaudion
David Geary
Amro Gebreel
Alexander Geissler
Lee Gelson
Alessandro Gentili
Benjamin George
Luca George
Theodoros-Franz Gerakitis
Joseph Giammarco
Elliott Gibb
Joseph Giblin
Patton Gilbert
Liam Gill
Arden Gini
Prentis Gipson
Ryan Girolamo
Markus Gissberg
Rob Glass
Chris Gloria
Alexey Glukhov
Michael Godfrey
GodOfTheMad
Jeffrey Golden
Nick Goman
Nuno Gomes
Lennart Grabowski
Trey Gracyalny
Joshua Graddick
Alex Mangor Grave
Nick Gray
Jeremy Grayson
Stuart Green
Gavin Greene
Kevin Greene
Richard Greene
Leo Greer
James Gregory-Monk
Carey Griffiths
Theodore Griffiths
Christopher Grimshaw

Jordan Grodecki
Kevin Groll
Zac Gunnell
Joseph Gusmorino
Ryan Gustman
Alan Guyan
Eric Gwaltney
Matthew Gyure
Steve 'Darc' H.
Colby Haag
Christopher Hable
David Haddow
Bryan Hadley
Elijah Hagberg
    (TheDarkMage)
Viktor Hägg
Haitani
Imdat Hakbilen
Badr Hakeem
Brian Halford
Jonathan Hall
Matthew Hall
Michael Hall
Timothy Halloran
Niall Halsall
Mark Halse
Will TwistdRabbit Hamilton
Casey Hampsey
Shawn Hanak
James Hanchett
Jeremy Hankinson
Michael Hardy
Dylan Harmon
David Harper
George Harper
The Harpoon
Caleb Harris
Emily Primrose Harrod
Justin Hartsell
Jen 'nuthin but a J thang'
    Harvey
Jonah Harwell
Thomas 'Covalent Arts'
    Harwood

Ingar Takanobu Hauge
Kyle Haugen
Luke Haugh
Spencer Hauldren
Aiden 'Ecto' Hawkins
Glenn Hawthorne
Matthew Hawthorne
Christian Hays
Sam Head
Reece Heather
Rebecca Heegaard
Jeffrey Heilbroun
Josef Heller
Dominik Hellmuth
Timothy Hely
Jordon Hempsall
David Henderson
Maick Hendrick
Tanner Henfey
Malte Henriksson
Danny Henry Jr
Lucy Henzell-Thomas
Taylor Herb
Mark Hermon
Cristopher Hermosilla
    Sánchez
Alexandro Hernandez
Mark C Hernandez
William Hernández
Héctor Hernández Aguilar
Cristofer Hess
Sam Heywood
Christian Hiesberger
Luke Higginbottom
John Hill
Taylor Hindman
Brandon Hines
Jack Hines
Oskar Hiorth
Michael Hoang
Josh Hogan
Michael Hohmann
Jacob Holdcroft
Niels Holkamp

Scott Holland
Ollie Holliday
Michael Hollinshead
Adam Holmes
Spencer Holmes
Jeremy Honaker
See Zheng Hong
Zanshlou Carmina Hood
Arthur Hooge
Ross Hooper
Rhiannon Hopkins
Josefina Hörberg
Oliver Horn
Logan Hornung
William Hoskins
Harold 'hh4hooch' Houchin
Anthony Hubbs
Liam Huckaby
Brian Huffman
Aaron P Hughes
Dave Hughes
Gareth 'Gonic' Hughes
Thomas Lloyd Hughes
Jens Humburg
Charlotte Hume
George Hume
Adam Humphreys
Kevin Hunter
Hubert Huon
Darren Hupke
Will Hurley
Samantha Hurrell
Jessica Hurtgen
HyliaKumatora
Vladimír Hýll
Nathan Hymas
@iamryancurtiss
Max Iarocci
Mikko Immonen
Wan Aly Imran
Sam Irwin
Abdulaziz Jabor
Jake Jackson
Jason Jackson

Sierra Jackson
Auke Jacobs
Daniel Jakobs
Alex James
Arfon James
Peter Janeczko
Wouter Janmaat
Marcus Jaxon
Michael Jay
Eric Jeffries
Christopher Jelle
Rob Jenkins
Jeremy Jennings
Rayan Jibril
Jid Jip
Ricky Johnson
Tyler Johnson
Brian Jones
Chase Jones
Daniel Jones
Emrys Jones
Garyl Jones
Jesse Jones
Lindsay Jones
Nathan Jones
H.C. Joseph
Tud Joshy
Duncan Joyce
Toch Jpgr
JunkSolution759
Piotr Jura
Edward Jurina
Jyoshiki
KaiKabuki
Karl F. Kaltenhauser
Brett Kampf
Chris Kane
Ohad Kanne
Michael Kaplan
Viktor Karasev
Kim-André Karlsen Rudolfsen
Fredrik Karlsson
Cory Karpinsky
Alex Karr

Devin Kasprowicz
Aaron Kauhn
Daniel Keay
Jamie Keenan
Colin Keil
Joann Kelleher
David L. Kelley
Joshua Kelley
Grant Kelly
Sean Kelly
David Kemp
Matthew Kempe
Dion Kennedy
Marcus Kennedy
Troy Kennedy
Colt Kerekes
Nick Kerkhof
Markus Keuschnig
Dan Kieran
John Paul Kilcrease
Jay 'Ronin Op F' Kim
Jin Kim
Thomas Kim
Lara Kindermann
Sawyer King
Tyler King
Will King
Elliott 'Kip' Kipper
LucaLink [Kirameki]
Alexander Kirchner-Wilson
Sam Kirkham
Kyle James Kirkpatrick
Maximilian T. Kister
James Klein
Drake Klemme
Joe Klotz
Krysta Kluge
Aodren Knight
Vincent Kocks
Wayne Koh
Madhav Korimerla
John Kozlowski
Bob Kozono
Bret Kragh

Amanda Kramer
Joel Kreutzwieser
Sebastian Kristiansen
Ashley Kronebusch
Holger Krupp
Andrew Kukulka
Alexander Kula
Matthew Kuzio
Luke Labishak
Mikayla Lack
Ionuț Lala
Josh Lambert
Jared Lance
Brian Lang
Kevin Lang
Jason Langdon
Matthew Langston
Dominic Laoutaris-Brown
Cyle LaPread
Aaron Larson
Avery K. Latta
Ronald Lauria
Casey Lawler
Matthew Lawley
Jack Layman
Alisha Le Sauvage
Ryan Ledbetter
Jon Ledford
Jonathan Lee
Padraig Leen
Patrick Lefebvre
LegionLx
Ethan Lego
Warren Leigh
Rodney Lelah
Rob Lennon
Trevor Leong
Eli Lete
Jonathan Lett
Brennan Lewis
Brian P. Lewis
Christopher Lewis
Ryan H Lewis
Warren Liang

Abraham Liao
Mario Liebisch
John Light
Besim Lika
Jaryl Lim
Mike Lindgren
Steven Lindquist
Sarah Lippmann
Francis Litwin
Kevin Liu
David Lloyd
Alexandra Logan
Sims Logan
Loki_The_Octo
Timothy, Emily, and
    Ami Rei Long
Joshua Lopez
Raul Lopez Orpez
Thorbjørn Lotsberg
Daniel Lowbridge
David Lua
Théo Lucas
Ralph Lucas III
Egon Lucic
Jonathan Lueck
Jose Miguel Vicente Luna
Elijah Lundby
Tyson Luschinski
Ramon Lux
Evan Lybrand
David Lyons
James M
Alexander Macdonald
Wilson MacDonald
Liam Mackenzie
Travis Mackin
Jeppe Vognsgaard Madsen
Luke Maglio
Joey Magnuson
Kassandra Magnusson
Logan Mahan
Sean Malatesta
Natalio Maldonado
Rick Mallen

Philip Mallett
Sam Manojlovic
Marden
Robbie 'DurradonXylles'
    Maresh
Nicholas Marinello
mariomont92
Darrik Marion
Craig Marler
Rodolfo Marques
Lorenzo Marras
David Marrero Jr
S Marshall
Brandon Marth
Thomas A. Martin II
Abel Adan Martinez
Ash Martinez
Diego Martinez
Reileigh Martinez
Ruben Martinez Jr.
Conrad Martinez Lambert
Xavier Marugan Ferrer
Steven Maruszak
Archie Maryon
Scott Mason
Jonathan Massey
Brendan Mathews
Michael Mathieu
MatrixMorpher
Edgar Mauleon
AJ Mazur
Dwayne Bernell McAfee Jr.
Christopher McBride
Grace McCarthy
Nick McCarthy
Jonathan McCartney
Craig McCauley
Joel McCleary
Sam McDonald
Stephen McEachern
Connor McElhinny
Braiden McFarland
Jesse McGough
Scott McGuire

Paul McGurk
James McIntyre
cAshleigh McJewin
Shawn McManus
Dave McVay
Jonathon Medina
Nick Mellish
Charles 'Dark CEPM 42'
    Melnyk
Mem-Sama (Mohammad
    Al-Dabbous)
Ryan Menge
David Michael Mensch
Andrew Meunier - Ku Kupo!!!
Aymeric Meuree
Mexiun
Brett Meyers
Arthur Mezzo
Anthony Micari
Chelsea Michel
Walter Michelin
Flo Mihola
Brian Miller
Daniel Miller
Rob Miller
Ryan Miller
Spencer Miller
Andrew Milliman
Andrea Millow
Bryan Mitchell
John Mitchinson
Edmund Miyashiro
Julian Molina
Jens Mollen
Colin Monsma
Justin Montana
Andrew Moore
Blake Moore
Mike Moore
Robert Moore
Shawn Moore
Anthony Morales
Fabian Morales
James Moran

Bill Morefield
Zachary Morehouse
Michael Morejon (Samuru)
Brady Morgan
Brian Morgan
Grant Morgan
David Morley
Joseph Morley
Chris Morris
Nathaniel Morris
Sean Morris
Sean Morrissey
Thomas 'Draken' Mortimer
Motrax
Mike Mücke
Joerg Mueller-Kindt
Tyson Muir
Efim Mulayev
Steve Mullers
David Munoz
Florian Münstermann
Hagen Munter
Teague Murphy
Andrew Murray
João Murtinheira
Matthew Mustovich
Matt Myers
Michael Myrick
mzx666
Christopher Nagle
Raj Nagra
Benjamin Nash
Philip Nash
Luuk Nass
Carlo Navato
Christopher Neale
Jason Neifeld
David Nelms
Peter Nelson
Amit Netanel
Matt Nevins
Joseph Newman
Gon Ng
Jonathan Ngo

Emily Nguyen
Paul Nguyen
Jim T. Nguyen (Makyuu)
Kyle Ryan Nickerson
Andrew Nicklin
Brady Nielsen
Igor Nikitin
Chris Niosi
Joe Nix
Benjamin Nordin
Lucinda Norman
Adam Notman
Coral Nulla
Thomas Nunn
Luke O'Connor
Mark O'Neill
Bryan O'Sullivan
Robert O'Sullivan
Lena Oakes
Alexandra S. Oberle
Jason Obermeyer
Pablo Ocares
Joseph Odenwald
Corey Ogburn
Kristoffer Ogint
Andrew Oliveira
Olly
Alexander Olson
Joshua Olson
Steve Olynyk
Nils Oostendorp
Mohamed Orekan
Shai Oren
Christopher Ortiz
Joseph Ortiz
Eric Oswald
Chris Ovak
OVchron
Alex Overton
Frank P.
Luís Pacheco
Amir Padan
Christian Page
Alex Palmer

Craig Palmer
Luke Palmer
Abdul Paniagua
Steven Pannell
Ryan Panske
James 'D-Boy' Panto
Zisis Paraskevaidis
Marjorie Pare and
   Alex Harvell
Arron Parkin
Ryan Parnas
Ashley-Ben Parsons
Don Parsons
Jamie Stuart Robin Parsons
Lex Patricio
Joshua Pattison
Cornelius Patzinger
Lillian Paul
Justin Pauls
Justin RH Payne
William Pearcy
Callum Pears
Ben Pease
A. J. Pecanic
Fabrizio Pedrazzini
Miguel Angel Perez Martinez
Slobodan Peric
Natalie Perkowski
Jonatan Petler
Lewis Petty
Lars Pfaff
Simon Phaneuf
Anthony Piccirillo
Uwe Pieper
Kaleb Pierotti
Götz Piesbergen
Pimp Daddy Love Muffin
Molly Pinegar
Steven Pinero
Maurizio Pistelli
Emily Pitts
Maximilian Pitz
Jack Plissken
Gregory Poblete II

Ford Polia
Justin Pollard
Stavros Polymenakos
John Pope
Amir Porat
Jacob Portelli
Christopher Potts
Sean Povey
David Powell
James Powell
Robin Powell
Grant Prasher
Jonjo Presland
Michael Pressburg
Luis Pringle
Kevin Pryke
Michael Pugliese
Joseph Pullen
Raine Pultz
Puma88
Joey Purvis
Daniel Quasar
Laura Quin
Stephen Quinlan
Torin Quinlivan
Ruben Quintas
Gavi Raab
Doug Raas
Alex Rackow
Byron Rademacher
Stuart Radley
Niels 'Nukem' Raemaekers
Jonathan Raftery
Dane Rainbird
Jack Rainsford
Tigas Ralha
Jessica Ramey
Ezekiel Ramirez
Eric Ramocki
John Ramsay
Dylan Randall
Armando Rangel
Brandt Ranj
Janosch Raschegewski

Jaymin Rau
Anthony Raymond
Samer Rayyan
Stephen Reading
Bill Reed
Richard Reese
James Reid
Matt 'Kosheh' Reinhardt
Thibaut Renaux
Enriquez Renteria
Retrogamershaun
Marvin Rhodeman
Maik 'ADarkHero'
   Riedlsperger
Tanner Riess
Austen Rietveld
Gregg Riley
Michael 'Soveskog' Riley
Steven Ripes
Mark Ritzman
Monica Akemi Riu
Horacio Rivera
Tim Rivera
Xavier Rivera
César Augusto Rivera P.
Matthew Robb
Izac Roberts
Joseph Roberts
Shayne Robins
Fergus Robinson
Frederik Robinson
X Robles
Tyler Rockwell
Marvin 'Niphram' Rode
Andy J Rodriguez
Michael Rodriguez
Rene Rodriguez
Skyler Rogers
Stephan Rohbäck
Armando Rojas
Danski Romanski
Garry Rooney
Aubrey Root
Espen Rørtveit

Matt A. Rosado
Luis Rosas
Eric Rosbough
Kjell Johan Rosenberg
Adam Rosenfield
Deacon Ross
Aaron Roth
Hannah Rothman
Roucasse
Martine Rousseau
Stephen Rowley
Thomas Ruddle
Alex Rudolph
RufUsul
Adam Rushing
James Rushmer
Liam Ryan
Nicholas Ryan
Zach Ryan
David Ryoo
Matthew Sager
Alex Saladrigas
Fox Salazar
Mikko Salovaara
Daniel Saltzmann
Jonathan Sammons
Ryan Sanchez
Marcus Sandberg
David Sandry
Bernardo Santos
Miguel Sarmento
Joseph Sauber
Becky 'glitchsaur' Saunders
Joshua Saunders
Scott Saunders
Savescreen
Todd Sayre
Alessandro Scapin
Derek Schaaf
Marco Scheerhoorn
Andreas 'Yeah' Scheidl
Robert Schmatzer
Karl Schmidt
Austin Schmitt

Matthew Schott
Sheldon Schrader
Josh Schreuder
Christopher Schumacher
Cameron Scott
George Peter Martyr Scott
Christopher Scott-Blore
From, Scry Studios
Paul Scullion
Ryan Seguin
Saphrone Willard
    James Seidel
Seiya
Elegardo Serrano
Alberto Serratos
Karsten Sethre
Chris Seto
Slawa Sewergin
Jonah Shafran
Mahmood Shaikh
Scott Shanbom
Alec Sharkey
Brandon Sharp
Dylan Shaw
Richard Shaw
Mark Shearn
Robeena Shepherd
Mark Sherman
Sherry
Wesley Shiflet
David Shine
Stephen Shiu
Christian Shortt
Thomas Shrum
Ricky Siddek
Alex Sieland
Verum Sileo
Leonardo Silva
Manuel Silva
Andy Sima
Josh Simmons
Daniel Simon
John Simpson
Jeff Sinclair

Benjamin Sinkula
Antonio Sirica
Spencer Sivertson
Christian Skipper
Mateusz Skoczylas
SlyFoxGamer
Dr. Smashface - He'll cure
    you or smash your face
Jack Smerdon
Joshua Smith
Robert Smith
Thomas M. Smith
Will Smith
Zachary M. Smith
Gunnar Smits
Ben Snowden
Kyle Andrew Snyder
Roberto Solares
Christopher Solis
Toby Solly
SomeRandomAxolotl
Max Somers
Samir Sookhan
JJ Soracco
Jesse Sosa
Heidi Sosinski
Alison Southern
Benjamin Spence
Alex Spivak
Dennis Spreen
Henry Springer
Spyperion
Mike Spysschaert
Jack Stack
Christopher Stacy
Sam Stafford
Sean Stafford
Kevin Stallings
Joe Stalsberg
Raymond Standen
Gry Stangnes
Wayne Stankewicz
Matt Stankiewicz
Skunk Starlight

Brett Starling
Michael Starnawski
Alexander Stasjulevich
Nathan Stazewski
Dustin Stebe
Connor Stec
Edward Stephenson
Patrick Stergos
Mark Stevens
Star Stevenson
Jim Stirrup
Matthew Stogdon
Vlad Stoiculescu
Christopher Stone
Chris Strater
TJ Strenger
Cloud Striker
Stephen Strini
David Stutter
Aaron Styles
Daniel Suarez
Ervin Sukardi
Sukiaki96
Daniel Sullivan
Zachary Sullivan
sumurtugu
Wayne Sung
Sami Suominen
Superjustinbros
Lida Supernaw
Alex Sushil
Tim Suter
Alex Nicole Sutherland
Scott Swank
Raelyn Sweanor
Patrick Swindler
James Sykes
Bryan Szatapski
Michael Szenay
Nulani t'Acraya
Justin Talentino
Alberto Talini
Erdinc Tarakci
Niall Tatton

Gianluca Tavola
Allen Taylor
Jack Taylor
Elephterios Tdc
Faure Teggin
Marcel Teller
Scheris Tennison
Christopher Testa
Jannes Thiele
Devontay Thomas
Gage Thomas
Dustin 'Pip' Thompson
Matthew Thompson
Molnár 'illesnagyapo' Tibor
John Tiglias
Brandon M. Tipton
Michael To
Alex Toader
Zakary Tober
Max Todd
Ari Torbin
Adonis Torres
Jacob Torres
Guillermo Torres Jr
Chris Townsend
Traumblebert
Trixie
Daniel Truax
Rebecca Tupas
Jake Turk
Robert Turner
Tamir Tuvel
Robert Tyler
Michael Ulrich
Trevor Ulrich
Daniel Umberger
Rowan Upstone
Gerard 'Peru' Urrutia
Alejandro Valdez
Joep Van de Wouw
Danilo van den Beemt
Frank van den Boogaard
Patrick van der Ende
Anthoinette van der Hurk

Jeroen van der Velden
Vincent van Ingen
Roland van Lin
Stef van Lin
Brad Van Orman
Martin Van Slett
Ezra Vance
Didier Vandenbil
Clifford Vanichsarn
Remy Varannes
Vijay Varman
Gilvan Vasconcelos
Kyle Vaughn
Ali Vazquez
Freddy Velasquez
Venti
Philip Ventura
Alberto Vera
Jonathan Vergara
Jim Verhoeven
Daniel Vetter
VGS_
Geo Villa
Anthony Villanueva
Dave Vincent
Vivithegr8
Nico Vliek
Parker Vockeroth
Justin Voelkel
Frank Volders
Justin Voss
Christopher Vossen
Crystal Vu
Javon Vu
Randy Vukov
Justin Wager
Peter Waghorn
Kyle Wahlstedt
David Wakat
Mike Waldron
Ivo Walhout
Eric A Walker
Mike Walker
Paul Walker

Branden Wallen
JP Walsh
JJ Wanda
Andrew Wantula
Jacob Ward
Rachel Ward
Bartosz Warzywoda
Anthony R Washington
Peregrine Wayman
Michael Weaver
Taylor Webb
Thomas Weber
Harald Weiand
Jamie Weir
Mike Weissberg
Bernard Welsh
Joe Wescott
Hugo Westgren
Jason Wetherbee &
    Calvin Bystedt
Andy White
Forester White
Lewis White
Nicholas White
Paul White II
John White III
Zachary Whiteside
Daniel Whitfeld

Duncan Whitford
(Rawr!)Licia Whittington
Jack Whitton
Liam Wilbor
Patrick Wilde
Fredrick Wildgoose
Joseph Wilhelm III
Tom Wilkin
Joseph Wilkins
Allen Willan
Cory Williams
Darksilverjesse Williams
Jimmy Williams
Tevin T.J. Williams
Tristan Williams
Brady Wilson
Stewart Wilson
Taylor Wilson
Noah Wise
Cody Wisinger
Joel Witts
Sander Woestenburg
David Wofford
Joseph Wojciechowski
Ian Wolf
Matthew Wolf
James Wood
Josh Wood

Justin Wood
Zach Wood
Dean Woodhouse
Ryan Woodhouse
Matt 'Woody' Woodward
Trevor Wooten
A Wylie
Chris Y
Andrew Yamamoto
George Elie Yazbeck
Adam Yeats
Raymond Yee
Jesse Yeh
Drew Young
Steve Young
Gavin Youngberg
Nicholas Yuan
zabbas
Jon Zalot
David Zell
Luwei Zhang
Benjamin Ziebert
Philipp Ziedler
ZRAMN
Jon Zrostlik
Seth Zubatkin
Andrew Zur
ゴゴゴ ゴゴゴ